Discerning
the Call

A PROJECT ON ENLISTMENT TO MINISTRY
Produced by
THE DIVISION OF HIGHER EDUCATION
On behalf of
THE CHRISTIAN CHURCH (DISCIPLES OF CHRIST)
Funded by
THE LILLY ENDOWMENT, INC.
1991

Discerning the Call

Advancing the Quality of Ordained Leadership

Edited by

John M. Imbler
and
Linda K. Plengemeier

Chalice Press
St. Louis, Missouri

© Copyright 1992 by Chalice Press

All rights reserved. No part of this book may be reproduced without written permission from Chalice Press, P.O. Box 179, St. Louis, MO 63166-0179.

Cover design: Will Hardin

John M. Imbler is Vice President for Theological Education of the Division of Higher Education, Christian Church (Disciples of Christ) and Director of the Project, *Advancing the Quality of Ordained Leadership*, funded by the Lilly Endowment, Inc.

Linda K. Plengemeier is Treasurer and Corporate Secretary of the Division of Higher Education, Christian Church (Disciples of Christ) and Associate Director of the Project, *Advancing the Quality of Ordained Leadership*, funded by the Lilly Endowment, Inc.

Library of Congress Cataloging-in-Publication Data

Discerning the call : advancing the quality of ordained leadership/ edited by John M. Imbler and Linda K. Plengemeier.
  Includes bibliographical references.
  1. Christian Church (Disciples of Christ)—Clergy—Appointment, call, and election.   2. Pastoral theology—Christian Church (Disciples of Christ)   I. Imbler, John M.   II. Plengemeier, Linda K.
BX7326.D49   1992   253   92-1111
ISBN 0-8272-0618-6

Printed in the United States of America

Contents

Introduction	1
Chapter 1 **Practical, Spiritual, and Intellectual Criteria for Ministry**	9
Chapter 2 **Ecclesiastical Linkages**	21
Chapter 3 **Congregational Enlistment**	37
Chapter 4 **Faith Development**	53
Chapter 5 **Changing North American Demographics**	79
Chapter 6 **Disciples Women in Ministry**	95
Chapter 7 **Characteristics for Success**	105
Afterword	111
Notes	121
Bibliography	129

Acknowledgments

Appreciation is expressed to the Lilly Endowment, Inc. of Indianapolis, Indiana, for recognizing the trends toward decline in seminary enrollments during the last decade. Even greater appreciation is expressed for the Endowment's willingness to help United States churches engage this situation by initiating the major grants program, "Improving the Recruitment and Selection of Ministerial Candidates." Fred Hofheinz, Director of the Religion Program, has been extremely supportive and patient as we struggled with reporting procedures and grant modifications. Joe O'Neill, Consultant to the Lilly Endowment, has made himself readily available to assist with contents and answer those baffling questions that plague all grant writers. Their ongoing guidance was invaluable as we proceeded through some denominational complexities.

Steering Committee members Joyce Coalson, Clark Gilpin, John Foulkes, Lester Palmer, and Pete Smith, raised the critical questions that kept me on track. Although most of our work was done through telephone and by mail, each made helpful suggestions that allowed the first year's work to progress smoothly.

I am profoundly grateful to the thirty-four Study Team members whose efforts produced this book. They entered this project with trepidation but emerged elated. It is to the credit of the seven Team Leaders that team members enjoyed their tasks and felt reluctant to disband. Special thanks to leaders Don Browning, Brian Grant, Margaret Harrison, Kenneth Henry, Susanne Johnson, Daisy Machado, and Holly McKissick. Their dedication to this project was borne out by their energy in the midst of their own busy schedules.

While this book was still in a working stage, twenty-nine people enthusiastically responded to an invitation to spend three days at a Planning Conference to evaluate its contents. Their willingness to share ideas, experiences, and dreams around ministry aided greatly in refining a draft into a finished product which hopefully will prove beneficial to the whole church.

My colleagues on the staff of the Division of Higher Education exhibited their characteristically fine grace as I became more deeply involved in the research and writing this phase of the Grant. Pat Burris and Kathy Johnson answered numerous phone calls and prepared mailings. Lawrence Steinmetz offered direction and critique and picked up otherwise loose ends which gave me space. Jim Spainhower continues to give wise counsel while affording me wide latitude in decision-making. Linda Plengemeier's challenging questions and insightful editing helped maintain the project's integrity. In addition, her careful attention to financial details enabled me to focus on the program. Thanks, too, to Lorie Plengemeier, a junior at Texas Christian University, who gave up part of her summer to type and retype my marginal scribblings on drafts that had been submitted to me cleanly.

John M. Imbler
Project Director

Introduction

The story we want to tell was eloquently expressed by Janet Long in an issue of *The Disciple* magazine.

"Why don't you become a local church pastor?" That question posed to me over thirteen years ago, remains vivid in my memory. What a novel idea! The suggestion came as a revelation, a startling thought indeed, since I knew no clergywomen who served as pastors of congregations.

The late Dr. Richard Kenney, Professor of Religious Studies at Bethany College, was very matter-of-fact in his approach to the subject, making the idea sound natural. Dr. Kenney, my academic advisor and dear friend, detected my surprise at his question. "Could I do that?" I ventured skeptically.

"Why of course you can." Knowing my commitment to enter a church related vocation, he was helping explore the options. What he viewed as obvious had been obscure to me. He knew of my sense of call and of my personality and the match with pastoral ministry was clear in his mind.[1]

Discerning the call to ministry is central to this book which arose out of a major project administered by the Division of Higher Education of the Christian Church (Disciples of Christ), and Ms. Long's testimony describes one example of discerning the call. Although her story has many variations, the theme is the same...an undefined call to Christian ministry was felt, and a caring person of influence sensed that call and nurtured it. Until the question is posed directly, individuals may remain in a quandary about ways in which they can realize their interests in Christian ministry.

For the past decade, recruitment officers from the four Disciples affiliated seminaries, two divinity houses, and the seminary foundation[2] have met annually to share recruitment strategies, compare notes on institutional enrollments, and discuss the changing nature of theological education. Throughout these collegial meetings there was an openly expressed concern for the advancement of the church's ministry: Who is responsible for enlistment? Where are the prospects? How do we nurture them? These questions should not be interpreted as unduly self-serving, rather they reflect a deep interest in the general well-being of the Christian Church (Disciples of Christ) and its future professional ministry.

How do we approach the complex issues of ministerial enlistment and retention in systematic ways? Representatives from the Disciples related theological education institutions along with staff members of the Division of Higher Education and the Department of Ministry of the Division of Homeland Ministries tested ideas for a church-wide enlistment strategy that would support individuals in their attempts to discern the call.

Providentially in 1987 the Lilly Endowment, Inc., headquartered in Indianapolis, Indiana, announced a major grants program entitled "Improving the Recruitment and Selection of Ministerial Candidates." Divided into three tiers, this grants program allocated $5,000,000 to address a situation common to all mainline Protestant religious bodies in the United States as well as Roman Catholics and Jews. Tier I was designated for research, primarily by divinity schools and seminaries, with one year grants up to $20,000 each.[3] Tier II focused on defining more systemic problems faced by denominations, and award amounts ranged from $250,000 to $400,000 spread over a three year period. Tier III is managed by Lilly Endowment as resource money to provide consulting and testing services in support of the Tiers I and II projects in addition to publishing results.

This announcement presented precisely the opportunity the Christian Church (Disciples of Christ) needed. The Division of Higher Education, on behalf of the church and in collaboration with the seven affiliated theological education institutions, the Department of Ministry, and the Pension Fund, submitted the proposal "Advancing the Quality of Ordained Leadership" in the amount of $292,375. The Division was selected as one of thirteen awardees from a field of over fifty applicants.[4]

Drafting the grant proposal was challenging. Because of a non-creedal, congregational posture no distinctive ethos presented itself for the Christian Church (Disciples of Christ). We cherish the breadth of our theological positions which, while living in covenant, allows us flexibility in faith and practice. The lack of a distinctive ethos, however, does make for some uncertainty in approaching issues of concern effectively. Acknowledging the high quality of Disciples ministers in this and preceding generations, the purpose of this Grant was to enable us to revitalize, without necessarily replicating or reclaiming, what once was a strong enlistment to ministry program for the church as it moves into the twenty-first century. This effort also implies a desire to reestablish effective youth programming.

Context

Seminary enrollments are but one aspect of the church's health, albeit a significant aspect. The Pension Fund of the Christian Church in 1986 reported that 43 percent of its 4,502 member Disciples clergy were between 50 and 65 years of age.[5] This means that by the turn of the century this formidable group of ministers will have retired or be preparing for their impending retirements. *Yearbook* statistics for that same period showed Disciples Master of Divinity enrollments in accredited theological schools in the United States and Canada hovered around 500, fluctuating by about eight percent over a four year period.[6] Seminary enrollments are not sufficient to provide a new clergy corps to replace those who are retiring.

The situation of the church's ministerial leadership is complicated by factors more elusive than enrollment figures. Were it only a matter of numbers, this project would have taken a different approach. As the title suggests, though, the emphasis is on quality in ministry, and defining quality is in itself problematic.

The increase of second career people in seminaries over the past ten years has brought strength to the theological education communities and invaluable leadership experience to the congregations. However, with a median age of 33 years for Disciples seminarians, projected tenure in ministry is reduced from an average of 40 years to 26-30. Some observers might view this as beneficial to the overall health of the church's ministry. Akin to the influx of second career people is the notable increase in the number of women pursuing ordination.[7] Women bring skills to ministry that are biblically-based and congregationally-desired, but not many women have been accepted into the ministerial ranks.

New immigrant populations often come to North America with education and aptitudes for ministry but are not assimilated easily. Language, culture, and customs may hinder them from receiving full credentials within the Christian Church (Disciples of Christ) as our standards for ministry remain based on Anglo American criteria. Settled racial/ethnic peoples find white majority culture and customs a barrier, too. Racial/ethnic ministers, particularly in Black and Hispanic congregations, historically have not had the benefit of formal theological preparation -traditionally four years of undergraduate liberal arts study plus three years of seminary. For many it has not been practical; for others, it has not been desirable.

Furthermore, the Christian Church (Disciples of Christ) is characterized by small congregations. Approximately 40 percent of Disciples churches have fewer than 100 members. Many lack the financial resources to attract full-time, ordained ministers; others lack the sociological will to develop the necessary resources. Small churches located in proximity to higher education institutions have offered field education positions for undergraduate and graduate ministerial students, and, therefore, have functioned as both training grounds and stepping stones to larger ministries. Unquestionably, the employment of student ministers is a valuable contribution for churches to make, and experience has shown that these churches have been well served. But that is not the sum and substance of those congregations' existence. Those small churches situated away from schools are often served by lay bivocational ministers whose dedication to the gospel of Jesus Christ is exemplary.

Aware of a variety of influences bearing on the future of the church's leadership, the drafters of this Grant chose to explore the following five hypotheses for enlistment to professional ministry:

1. Enlistment for ministry will be enhanced by encounters with "pastor-mentors," whose vitality and professional excellence will mitigate the influence of cultural perceptions of the ministry. Unlike older "Timothy" programs, we should not assume that the mentor will necessarily or even usually be the candidate's local pastor.

2. Enlistment for ministry will be enhanced by the experiences of the life and work of the church beyond the local congregation in wider social and cultural settings. Such experiences introduce both the rich diversity of ministry and its stimulating ethical and intellectual challenges. Such experiences reinterpret the opportunities of congregational ministry by placing them within the broader context of the church's life.

3. Enlistment for ministry will be enhanced when outstanding persons "enlist each other." They need to be brought together for common inquiry into the possibilities of ministry.

4. Enlistment for ministry will be enhanced by critical appropriation of current research on faith development and the processes of career decisions.

5. Enlistment for ministry will be enhanced by persuasive, yet realistic, presentations of the career opportunities for persons of different ages, races, and genders. This will entail broad ecclesial commitment to the renewal of ministry and a major education/interpretation venture with congregations and regions.

In developing these hypotheses, it was carefully determined that while we recognize the contributions and qualities brought to ministry by second career people, the project would focus on 12 to 22 year old male and female Disciples who are considering options for their first careers. And, though valuing the importance of the small churches and the dedicated bivocational ministers who serve them, the scope of these hypotheses required us to concentrate on the church's full-time ordained ministry. These were not judgments of exclusion but a decision of manageability.

Procedures

Upon notification of grant approval, the initial step was the selection of a steering committee to oversee the project and offer counsel at various stages of its implementation.[8] This Committee was large enough to represent the Disciples various constituents in ministerial nurture, yet small enough to be efficient. One of its first tasks was to appoint leaders for the seven study teams defined in the Grant. The purpose of each study team will be described in turn, but the overall charge was "...partnership in the task of advancing the quality of ordained leadership in the Disciples of Christ. Within that task all Study Teams are asked to provide research, analyze data, generate ideas, and propose strategies, bearing in mind that the Christian Church (Disciples of Christ) expresses itself in three manifestations and is characterized by diversity in culture, gender, age, size, and location."

In preparing the grant proposal, it was discovered that much information peculiar to the Christian Church (Disciples of Christ) was not available, particularly on racial/ethnic minorities. It was learned, also, that some information was available on ministry but was scattered. Finally, it became apparent that some critical questions relative to the church's ministry had never been raised. Each study team was instructed to create, compile, or in other ways develop relevant materials that would provide a useful resource for the church. This volume represents that compilation of research and analysis.

The reader will discover an unevenness in length and style from chapter to chapter. Each team leader was given only general guidelines for the preparation of the written reports having been instructed

6   *Discerning the Call*

to use as much or as little ink and paper as was necessary to present the findings. The unevenness also results from the nature of each group's assignment. For two groups, charts and graphs proved helpful; three used survey instruments, and two others prepared straight narratives. The unevenness, however, should in no way lessen the impact of what each has to say.

Also the reader will notice that the rationales and recommendations often are duplicated from one report to another, and in some instances conflict with each other. While there were two team leaders' meetings for consultation and clarification, each team functioned independently, approaching its work from its particular perspective. It was a conscious editorial decision not to rewrite these reports for the sake of conformity of style. Since all seven consumed more than a year's work, each has integrity unto itself. The richness of language preserves the unique contributions of each team member and the distinctive character of each team. The contents, whether duplicate or contradictory, reflect some of the best Disciples thinking on the nature of the church and its ministry.

Chapter Summaries

Chapter One[9] sets an important context in seeking to identify the practical, spiritual, and intellectual criteria desired by the church for its ministry in the coming age. By describing the social milieu in which the church functions, the team agreed that the term "spiritually empowered practical theologian" presents an ideal image for professional leadership.

Chapter Two[10] focuses specifically on the ecclesiastical linkages of the Christian Church (Disciples of Christ). There is much information available about the church's ministry, although it lacks centrality and coordination. Written policies and procedures are important, yet the practice of independent interpretation of such policies and procedures can lead to confusion.

Chapter Three[11] investigates the congregational or extra-congregational forces which influence people in the their decisions to consider professional ministry. Evaluation of those influences offers clues as to why certain congregations produce an unusually high number of ministerial candidates.

Chapter Four[12] addresses developmental theory by describing the interactions of youth cultures and adult cultures. Descriptions of youth ministry and the roles of youth in the church are presented in detail to set the context for why Christian ministry may or may not be seen readily as a career option.

Chapter Five[13] offers an analysis of the increasingly multicultural profile of the United States by tracking population shifts and immigration patterns. It explains the differences in expectations for ministry and the differences in ways religious experiences are corporately expressed in racial/ethnic communities.

Chapter Six[14] outlines the current situation of Disciples women in Christian ministry. Illustrations of the spiritual gifts and intellectual abilities exhibited by female seminarians demonstrate their capabilities to engage in the tasks of ministry.

Chapter Seven[15] begins to define Christian ministry in terms of success. Success in seminary, through intellectual ability, emotional stability, and positive spiritual development, indicates the potential for success in ministry. In addition there is need for an ongoing relationship between the church and the seminary in discerning and supporting ministerial candidates.

Each report has significant value as a reflection/action piece but is not intended to be the final word on the subject. Individuals, congregations, institutions, regions, and general administrative units of the Christian Church (Disciples of Christ) are invited to read each chapter carefully and to consider seriously the recommendations offered, with the understanding that at points alterations or adjustments may be necessary relative to particular situations. The distribution of this book does not constitute the completion of this project but rather its beginning as we work together to **Advance the Quality of Ordained Leadership.**

1

Practical, Spiritual, and Intellectual Criteria for Ministry

This chapter summarizes our reflections on the question of the spiritual, intellectual, and practical qualifications for the future ordained ministry of the Christian Church (Disciples of Christ). It weaves together and extends unpublished papers written by each of us on specific themes relative to our immediate task.

The ministry of the future must be simultaneously faithful to the gospel message of Christianity as well as responsive to the emerging social context of modern societies. It must entail both a vigorous and honest recovery of scripture and tradition as well as a commanding understanding of the forces that are shaping the modern world. More specifically, the retrieval of the ancient message will be rendered all the more vivid and powerful by the degree to which ministry poses questions to it out of a full confrontation with the dynamics of modern life. This is the hermeneutical circle so widely discussed in theological education today.

Contexts of the Future

There is much contemporary discussion about the emergence of a postmodern intellectual and cultural ethos, but there is little evidence that the actual dynamics of modernization are being attenuated. The single most dominant characteristic of modern societies has been, and promises to be, the relentless application of technical or purposive rationality to the satisfaction of human desires. Although Max Weber named this reality at the beginning of this century, the logic and actual working of technical rationality dates back to the later years of the Protestant Reformation and the early years of the Enlightenment.[16] There are many positive benefits associated with technical rationality such as increased wealth, modern medicine, and the ease and comfort of modern life.

The church should not pose as an enemy to technical rationality as such, even though some of its consequences are ambiguous. It is very likely, although not inevitable, that these trends will continue and accelerate. These include the increasing structural differentiation of secondary institutions and the declining influence of religion over these institutions; the increasing pluralization of society with proliferating interest groups, work groups, and life styles; the increase of privatistic forms of individualism; the decline of publicly shared meanings, including religious meanings; the further decline of institutional religion, especially of the liberal kind; a growing division between the rich and the poor with this separation being significantly determined by those who can and those who cannot make use of the tools of technical rationality; and increasing deinstitutionalization of the family, shifting gender roles, and a growing demand for autonomy and equality in male-female relations. This list of trends is common to societies that make technical rationality central to their cultural projects whether or not they be Marxist or liberal democratic in social philosophy.

Recent events suggest that huge sections of the Marxist world are turning toward democratic and economic liberalism. This reality, as welcome as it is, may accelerate all the trends above and add at least two more. These include, first of all, the spread across the world of the consumerism that the marriage of technical rationality and economic liberalism has tended to encourage. Second, it entails the increasing pollution of the earth and atmosphere that is a by-product of the industrial machinery that consumerism demands in either the socialist or capitalist contexts. The human tendency toward anxiety, sin, and guilt will both fuel and rigidify these dynamics just as they had much to do with creating the human project that spawned them. The cultural goal of satisfying human desire through technical rationality is problematic primarily because it is idolatrous and overdetermined. In this, it is implicated in the structure of human sin.

Although, as we have said, the church's ministry of the future should not pose as the enemy of technical rationality as such, that ministry will need to understand and address the world created by our relentless and idolatrous overreliance on it.

Preserving and Deepening Past Accomplishments

In what follows, we are assuming the validity of some well-established trends, i.e., that ordained ministers should be well-educated, should include both men and women, and should be racially and ethnically diverse. We assume that the most fundamental need will be in congregational ministry. But we also assume there will be a need for a variety of specialized ministries in institutional chaplaincy, pastoral counseling, campus ministry, administration, missions, and social service.

It is especially important to preserve, deepen, and extend trends toward cultural, ethnic, and racial pluralism in the ordained ministry of the Christian Church (Disciples of Christ). The increasing presence of Asian and Hispanic groups in the United States, the importance of African-American groups, and the presence of other racial/ethnic minorities demands a concerted effort to prepare an ordained ministry to meet the needs of these populations. Several of the reports that follow will stress the importance of ordained ministry with these groups.

The Minister as "Spiritually Empowered Practical Theologian"

The image of the ministry that we propose is summarized by the idea of minister as a "spiritually empowered practical theologian." Several recent proposals have emphasized the image of the minister as practical theologian or practical theological thinker.[17] We intend to balance these proposals with a strong emphasis on the need for the minister to be a *"spiritually empowered* practical theologian." This image of ordained ministry would replace, although certainly still include, recent dominant images of the minister as manager, therapist, or social activist.

The trends produced by technical rationality often invoke a profound sense of loneliness, insecurity, and emptiness in the hearts of modern individuals and societies. From our perspective, this suggests a deepening sense of the absence of God from human affairs. For many this translates into a sense of casualness and cynicism about life and a lack of seriousness about its possibilities. Helping to create a deeper sense of the reality and presence of God in the church, among its youth, and in the world beyond is the ministry's first and most important contribution to the spiritual hunger and turmoil that accompanies modernity. For ministers to help create a sense of the presence of God in congregations, they must exhibit a sense of this presence in their own lives. Yet this spirituality must not end in privatism and retreat from the world; it must empower a new kind of practical theological reflection and action that can lead to the reconstruction and revitalization of modern experience.

The image of the minister as "spiritually empowered practical theologian" entails some of the following considerations:

1. *There needs to be a fresh appropriation of the spiritual traditions of the Bible, Christian history, and the traditions of our Disciples heritage.* Jack Suggs pointed out that the New Testament qualifications for leadership must be understood within a time framework that distinguishes between an early popular phase and a later formal or institutional phase. He suggests that in the early popular stage of the Christian movement, leadership was charismatic— based on compelling, essentially self-authenticating qualities which gave one standing and authority. This was the central qualification for leadership put forth by Paul. During this period, the language of "call or appointment or commission by God" was also emphasized. Although the difference may be subtle, the popular period has produced criteria by which leaders are *recognized* while in the formal and institutional stages the criteria function to determine *eligibility* for office. In the later formal stage, it is important to observe that the language of spirituality and call persists but is significantly augmented by more "objective" criteria such as integrity and high moral principles (1 Tim. 3:2, 3:10; Tit. 1:6-7), temperance and sobriety (1 Tim 3:2, 3:11; Tit. 1:7-8), monogamous faithfulness (1 Tim. 3:2, 3:11-12; Tit. 1:6), wise household management (1 Tim. 3:4, 3:5, 3:12, Tit. 1:6), both maturity in the faith (1 Tim. 3:6) as well as the capacity to teach its central doctrines (1 Tim. 3:2; Tit. 1:9), and a baseline personal ethic consistent with the central moral values of the Hebraic tradition as well as broadly accepted by pagan culture (Tit. 3:9).

The emphasis on spirituality was central to both the contributions of William Paulsell and William Fox. Following Nelson Thayer, Fox defined spirituality as how we experience ourselves in relation to what we designate as the source of ultimate power and meaning in life, and how we live out this relationship. Paulsell believes that a minister should have an interest in religious experience and reminded us that a people's values, ethics, life styles, and commitments are grounded on their knowledge of God or lack thereof. But he also holds that the minister should be aware of the relation between spirituality and social activism and not assume that an interest in one cancels an interest in the other.

One cannot advance the image of the minister as a "spiritually empowered practical theologian" without observing that the language of spirituality has not always been thought to be central to the Disciples heritage. But this is so only if spirituality is given a narrow, privatistic, individualistic, and overly emotional meaning. Although Disciples have not been given to emotionalism, they have been inclined toward what Ronald Osborn has called a "full-orbed spirituality." By this he means "a genuine relationship with God which controls all one's intentions, spirituality integrated with the life of the mind, the intent of the will, the affections of the heart, and the use of one's bodily energies." This kind of spirituality will "manifest itself in openness to and loving concern for the persons one encounters in one's own experience and as commitment to the well-being of all people everywhere in justice and peace."[18] It is our belief that this kind of spirituality has been a central feature of the Disciples tradition and is a fundamental qualification for ministry.

2. *The minister as spiritually empowered practical theologian must understand theologically and intellectually the relation of Christian spirituality to practical theological reflection and action.* Practical theological reflection attempts to both describe and reconstruct the contemporary experience of both the Christian community and the secular world. It does this in response to the fragmentations created by the interaction of human sin with the dynamics of modernity. Christian ethics is central to theological reflection, but practical theology is more than moral thinking narrowly defined. Practical theological reflection entails the constant reworking of our religious concepts, our image of the world, and our image of self and society in light of the challenges, changes, and threats of contemporary experience.

Christian theology and Christian spiritual experience provide an essential framework for practical moral reflection. They contribute an understanding of a God that affirms the goodness and seriousness of human life; the idea that all humans are made in the image of this God and are therefore of infinite value (and therefore not to be manipulated, oppressed, or harmed); the view that this God is just, and both supports and measures all finite instances of justice; and the concept that this God, through Christ, is the source of all forgiveness and grace that both frees us and empowers us to overcome our moral failures and pursue again the peace and justice of God's realm. The minister of the future must understand that Christian theology is not just a nice addition to practical moral reflection. It is an essential contribution that both empowers and fulfills our moral thinking.

This deeper understanding of the relation of Christian thought to practical moral thinking should entail a profound grasp of the interaction of the Hebrew prophetic and wisdom traditions and the Greek traditions of moral philosophy within the spiritual breakthroughs of primitive Christianity. And the minister must understand the continuing interaction of these traditions throughout Western history. Nothing less than this is required if the Christian minister is to become a spiritually empowered practical theologian. This means listening more carefully to the New Testament, to insure explication of early Christian images of spiritually powerful leadership in terms of their shaping by Judaism's images of prophet, sage, and rabbi and by Hellenism's images of the moral philosopher.

3. *Ministers of the future must have the skills to actively lead in the creation of communities of spiritually empowered practical theologians.* It is not just ordained ministers who should be "spiritually empowered practical theologians;" they should help create congregations and religious communities full of Christians with these gifts and capacities. The minister as *spiritually* empowered practical theologian must know how to lead in the creation of communities of spirituality, communities of *interpretation*, communities of *practical religious reflection*, and communities of *action and service*. The emphasis here is not so much on the minister but on the communities that the minister helps create and sustain.[19] There is both theological and sociological support for this emphasis on the minister as active facilitator of communities of spiritually empowered practical reflection.

On the other hand, sociological research into the qualities of successful ministers emphasizes characteristics compatible with this image of the minister as active facilitator of spiritually alive communities of practical moral discourse and action. Sue Cardwell summarized some of the results of the "Readiness for Ministry" data reported in David Schuller's *Ministry in America*.[20] The capacities for the minister to have an "open and affirming style" and to "care for persons" were listed number one and two out of eleven central expectations that laity have for their ministers. Although these qualities flow directly from the theological understanding that all persons are children of God, the high value that the laity places on these characteristics may reflect a special feature of modern Protestant churches. In many ways they are voluntary institutions involved in open religious and moral discourse about the interpretation and reconstruction of the meaning of their lives in the world. For the minister to lead and sustain this hermeneutical conversation, she or he must be open, affirming, and caring.

The emphasis on the spirituality of the minister, however, greatly qualifies the meaning of "open and affirming." It is not just an easy style with people typical of the superficial warmth of our various commercial and therapeutic enterprises. It is an openness and affirmation based upon God's love for all people, even within the struggle of their moral deliberations with one another.

Third and fourth on the list were the expectations that the minister also be "theologically competent" and have a deep "personal commitment" to the faith. Cardwell also reports that on the specifically Disciples responses to the study, fourth on their list of valued qualities was the minister's capacity to integrate "life and thought" (especially the minister's own life) from the perspective of Christian theology. Disciples want their ministers to be both spiritually and theologically competent, but they also seem to want them to be practically minded people able to lead their congregations to relate faith to the common life.

4. *The Minister as the leader in creating communities of practical theological reflection and action provides the framework for understanding the specific practical skills required for the ministry of the future.* As stated earlier, this entails skills in creating communities of *spirituality, interpretation, practical moral reflection,* and *action and service.*

a) *A Community of Spirituality.* To create a community of spirituality, the minister must be adept in the disciplines of spirituality, first for himself or herself and then for others. This includes not only prayer and personal devotions but a keen sense of the liturgical traditions and expressions in worship of both the Disciples and the wider church. It also includes the development of a contemplative attitude in all of life. Fox has called our attention to the spiritual power of the African-American churches and suggests that Caucasian ministerial students be exposed to experiences in these churches. We affirm this suggestion along with Paulsell's proposal that Disciples ministerial students should study a variety of spiritual traditions with an eye to a critical appropriation of some of these resources.

b) *A Community of Interpretation.* To create a community of interpretation, the Disciples minister must be a superior interpreter of the texts of the Old and New Testaments and the cultural contexts that influenced the development of early Christianity. But the minister must also be a powerful interpreter of the contemporary world. In fact, it is the unique task of the minister as practical theologian to be able to interpret the classic Christian texts in light of questions that evolve from contemporary experience and, in turn, interpret this experience in light of the classic texts.

But these acts of interpretation are not simply the individual task of the minister. Ministers should help create these skills of interpretation in the religious communities they lead. *Preaching* and *teaching* are at the heart of this process. But for ministers to create communities of interpretation, preaching and teaching must entail listening and describing the questions of their congregations, bringing these questions to the scriptures, and in turn placing the scriptures in the hands of their congregations with the challenge that they be an integral part of the interpretive process.

c) *A Community of Practical Moral Reflection.* To create a community of practical moral reflection, the minister must be as interested in practical thought as he or she is in practical action. The contemporary call in the mainline churches for social action and witness is frequently impulsive and uncritical. Ministers should not always aim for direct action; it may be more important to raise the church's general capacity for competent moral reflection. The task of the minister of the future is to encourage a wider and deeper moral consciousness in the church. This may entail introducing churches to Christian forms of moral philosophy and a concern with method in Christian ethical thinking as background and preparation for addressing specific issues. Sometime people need distance from direct action and witness in order to grow in the skills of listening, interpreting, analyzing, sharing, and respectfully challenging one another as they take part in communities of practical theological and moral reflection. Churches need education in the art of moral discourse.

d) *A Community of Action and Service.* The minister must have skills in leading communities of witness, action, and service. Practical theological reflection has the final purpose of making our Christian lives more faithful in an increasingly more complex and threatening world. Practical theological reflection is not an end in itself. Its purpose is finally witness and transformation. The move from practical reflection to practical action is full of challenges, difficulties, and sacrifices. Our spirituality and mutual care is needed to sustain us in our action as well as to put it in proper perspective. The task of the church is not, however, to solve all the problems of life; the finitude and sin of human life mean that problems will always be with us. Our task, instead, is to exhibit a faith, an attitude, and an intelligent action that show forth God's concern, mercy, love, and justice in history and the affairs of humans. Practical theological reflection must engender action but an action that is primarily a witness to God's action.

Nonetheless, the church must attempt to address the destructive consequences of the subtle interplay between sin and a misdirected technical rationality. It must help create a new kind of public discourse designed to help give moral direction to technical rationality. It must find ways to direct technical rationality for the common good rather than for the satisfaction of the myriad of subjective desires that presently motivate and control its use. It must find ways to overcome the growing split between the rich who control technical rationality and the poor and uneducated who are either bewildered by it or have no access to its power and fruits. And the church must search, along with others, for ways to mitigate the ecological destruction, both sociological and environmental, that is presently a side effect of technical rationality.

In addressing these issues, however, ministers of the future should not see either themselves or their congregations as carriers of instant and certain solutions. They should see themselves as active facilitators of communities of practical theological discourse about the religious and ethical frameworks needed to address such issues. They should prepare themselves to be leaders of religious communities of practical discourse who will, in turn, become part of a society-wide process of ethical discourse. The church will not, by itself, solve these issues. There are technical aspects to all of these problems about which the church will need to learn from others. The church will bring unique religious and moral insights but few final solutions.

Ministers of the future must have skills to help churches bring forth in understandable form the witness and contributions of their unique historical tradition. These same ministers must have additional communicative and interpretive skills to deliver these special contributions to the wider deliberations of a pluralistic society that will never again simply reflect the opinions of a single religious tradition. Hence, the minister of the future must both help the church interpret the tradition as well as interpret the church's practical deliberations to the relevant centers of moral discourse in the wider society. The minister of the future must understand the ethics of discourse as an inextricable part of the ethics of action, both for the church and the larger society of which it is a part.

5. *The minister of the future must be a person of strong intelligence but must be, above all, creative.* It is our understanding that there is a continuing debate about whether or not the standards of intelligence of Disciples students preparing for ordained ministry has gone down or is remaining at a level consistent with earlier generations of ministers. According to Cardwell, there seems to be evidence supporting both sides of the issue. This debate seems important not because intelligence is a value that is, in itself, essential for Christian ministry but because intellectual abilities do seem to correlate with

creativity. Cardwell reports that when creative students and ministers were compared to students in general, creative ministers were five points higher and creative students were approximately seven points higher on the California Test of Mental Maturity than students in general. A certain threshold of intelligence seems to be necessary for creativity and adaptability.

The image of the minister as "spiritually empowered practical theologian" is complex and requires a capacity to correlate analyses of contemporary situations and people's individual questions with the resources of scripture and tradition. It will require both the skills listed above and a high degree of flexibility, creativity, and resilience. Since intelligence and creativity seem to correlate at least to some extent, it is important for the Christian Church (Disciples of Christ) to double its efforts to bring candidates of strong native intelligence into the Christian ministry.

6. For ministers to be spiritually empowered practical theologians, they must have special skills to analyze and interpret situations. Understanding and interpreting the gospel, of course, is central. But the practical theologian must relate the gospel to situations. Interpreting situations requires three things: 1) a vital concern with these situations, 2) an interpretation of situations from the perspective of the gospel, and 3) a description and interpretation of situations from the perspective of relevant social science disciplines. Ministers need tools to understand in basic ways the sociological, psychological, and economic infrastructures of society. This does not mean that ministers must be sociologists, psychologists, or economists. But it does mean that ministers must have skills in reading, using, and critically assessing these disciplines. This is important because the secular world, and large portions of our congregations, are increasingly understanding themselves and their worlds in light of the human sciences. The minister who cannot use and critically assess these disciplines will be powerless to relate the Christian gospel apologetically to these alternative interpretive perspectives.

7. Finally, the church needs to develop a new generation of spiritually empowered practical theologians to develop special ministries with youth. The issue of faith development is outside the special assignment of our task force. Nonetheless, we have developed a deep conviction that the church needs to give special attention to youth and young adults between the ages of 13 to 25. It is our contention that young people during this period have spiritual hungers the church is ignoring. At the same time, this group is particularly susceptible to attractions, movements, and ideologies that disparage the church. The minister as "spiritually empowered practical theologian" must have skills in stimulating and supervising ministries to this age group. It is our conviction that the combination of spiritual empowerment and practical relevance can be especially attractive to the youth of our society.

Proposals for Recentering Ministry

The significance of our proposals can be made clearer if they are contrasted with our perception of recent emphases in the ministry and in ministerial education. How the educator programs the development of these qualities is a matter of debate. Church leaders and theological educators, if they react favorably to our proposals, will have ideas about the means to accomplish these goals.

1. We consider ourselves emphasizing the qualities of the minister as active leader in contrast to the minister as relatively passive facilitator. When we do use the word facilitator, we couple it with the word "active" and speak of minister as "active facilitator." We believe that the phrase "active leadership" is even better and not incompatible with a leadership that encourages participation and initiative on the part of the laity.

2. Our emphasis on the practical does not exclude either the spiritual or the intellectual. In fact, we put heightened emphasis on both in contrast to recent images of the minister. Practical action on behalf of others requires a spiritual awareness of the status of all humans before God. Furthermore, practical thought and action require more rather than less historical, theological, and philosophical skills. The practical, in this context, does not mean short-term results; it means, instead, the development of a religious culture in the churches which helps build up both the life of the church and the common life of society over the long haul of history.

3. Our emphasis on the minister as practical theologian does not mean we believe the thought and skills of ministers and congregations alone will solve the problems of our society. We believe, instead, that this spiritually empowered practical thought and action most of all serves to both detect and witness to what God is doing in the midst of the church and human history.

4. Our emphasis on the practical is seen as a slight recentering of the role of the prophetic and the political in the church's ministry. We do not wish to back away from either. The church must always be willing to project a prophetic message. But this does not mean that the

church's ministry should be reduced to an endless series of direct social pronouncements and actions. The minister as practical theologian leading a community of practical theologians works to provide the critical tools and more mature capacities for the church's ongoing critical and appreciative responses to the society that surrounds it.

5. The emphasis on the minister as "spiritually empowered practical theologian" is not designed to downplay the importance of minister as preacher, liturgist, teacher, care giver, and administrator. It is, rather, to develop a new integrating center within which to locate and define these traditional offices. The skills of describing and analyzing concrete situations combined with the capacities to think both theologically and practically should strengthen the minister in the performance of all of these traditional roles.

6. Our emphasis on the capacities of the minister to appeal to youth and both inspire and supervise work with youth has implications for ministerial recruitment. Although the church should encourage gifted people at all stages of life to investigate ordained ministry, it is of crucial importance to have a core of young men and women who come into ministry early and who bring a broad and deep early experience with both the Christian Church (Disciples of Christ) and the larger ecumenical church.

2

Ecclesiastical Linkages

Ecclesiastical linkages within the Christian Church (Disciples of Christ), different from the more formal connections of other denominations, serve as a covenantal means of developing coordination and accountability. We undertook our task by reviewing the enlistment and under care processes as they involve laity, local pastors, regional staff, theological education institutions, campus ministries, and undergraduate schools. We tried to clarify our particular focus relative to the church structures by (1) identifying the entities that carry responsibility for recruitment, nurture, and training for ministry and (2) evaluating how effectively these components work together. This evaluation was based on ways in which the connections are perceived by those who execute the program, those who are affected by it, and evidence of the system as it actually works.

Methodology

We met twice in St. Louis, Missouri and once in Denver, Colorado with individual assignments completed between meetings. Generally the process that emerged included the following elements:

1. Information was gathered from relevant documents:
    Policies and Criteria for the Order of Ministry
    Regional Commissions on Ministry Policy Statements
    Reports and Minutes of the General Board's Task Force on Ministry
    Report of the 1988 Consultation on Black Ministry
    Various articles, reports, and studies of Disciples and others

2. Interviews by mail or in person were held with key individuals from ecclesiastical units:
    DHM Department of Ministry Executive DHE Vice President Task Force on Ministry Chair
    Several Regional Ministers

22   *Discerning the Call*

    3. Students in preparation for ministry were surveyed:
        Questionnaire to Disciples students in Disciples-related colleges and selected state universities
        Questionnaire to Disciples seminarians

We subsequently condensed our conclusions and analyses into four areas which form the outline for this chapter: (a) general and regional commissions on the ministry, (b) high school and post high school, (c) college and university, and (d) seminary. Narratives and recommendations are intentionally combined in each section to provide a clearer and more immediate reference to our conclusions.

Contents and Results of Inquiries

General and Regional Commissions on the Ministry

Observations:

- No single person or general administrative unit has oversight of a total program of recruitment and preparation for ministry.

- While important parts of such a program are carried by departments or various administrative units, the coordination is more a matter of individual contact and cooperation rather than a comprehensive, intentional plan.

- There has been a general decline in activities in which ministries of the church are presented and probable candidates identified (e.g. high school and college level camps, conferences, rallies, work camps).

- Few denominationally directed interpretive materials are available to aid local pastors, youth directors, campus ministers, and others in support of enlistment efforts.

- Most regional commissions on ministry documents are similar in their conformity with the *Policies and Criteria for the Order of Ministry* document.

- Actual functions of the regional commissions vary greatly. The major differences are between commissions in areas where Disciples-related colleges and seminaries are located and regions without Disciples-related educational institutions. Because of the proximity to affiliated schools, functions of commissions may be more refined due to the likelihood of serving more candidates.

- Regional commissions have no enlistment assignments. Their programs of "under care" begins after a person declares an intent to enter the ministry.
- The composition of the commissions, frequency of meetings, and contact with candidates varies from region to region. Movement of a person from one region to another often results in confusion of "who is responsible for what" in nurturing the candidate for ministry.

Recommendations

1. There should be a central "office" for coordinating policy-making and review, developing program materials, and compiling a comprehensive list of probable ministerial candidates for enlistment and training for ministry. This could mean that the General Board Task Force on Ministry would be elevated to a more regular, permanent status appropriately staffed to serve coordination, evaluation, administration, and other functions.

2. A common computer system should be in place to facilitate the identification, tracking, and sharing of information on candidates for ministry from local, regional, and general church sources.

3. Interpretive materials should be prepared to aid pastors, youth workers, and others who may enlist persons for ministry. Some of these materials need to refer to the particularities of Disciples structures relative to nurture and guidance.

4. The under care program of most regions needs clarification and, at crucial points, coordination across regional lines. The Oregon Plan is one of the best we observed.[21]

5. Some guidelines for the composition of a commission on the ministry should be developed to ensure that they are inclusive of regional staff, pastors, lay persons, and theological educators.

6. Opportunities should be utilized as fully as possible to interpret the roles of the commissions and administrative units concerned with enlistment and training by clearly affirming and supporting worthy candidates for ministry rather than presenting obstacles to fulfillment of their calls to ministry.

7. Special attention needs to be given to the post-high school non-college-bound group for potential candidacy for ministry involving local, regional, and general structures. The Christian Church in Ohio has accomplished this well through a structured post-high school conference.

24   *Discerning the Call*

The following table illustrates ecclesiatical responsiblities and opportunities for the Christian Church (Disciples of Christ):

POSSIBILITIES AND RESPONSIBLE
AGENTS FOR MINISTERIAL ENLISTMENT

High School Through Seminary

Responsible Agents	*Experiences/Programs*	*Changes Needed*
High School		
local pastors	General Assembly	camp image
key laity	regional assembies	conference image
scholarships	CYF camp	institutional
district and area structures	state youth conference	image of colleges
community role models	Week of the Ministry Christian ed curriculum	
College		
local pastors	General Assembly	list from home congregations
key laity	regional assemblies	affirming students
scholarships	campus ministers and chaplains	and coordination of that information
commissions on ministry	national student conferences	volunteer and job opportunities
DHE	STEEM	information and coordination
religion professors	Week of Ministry	
campus ministers and chaplains	congregational programs	
college town pastors		
Seminary		
local pastors	General Assembly	
key laity	regional assemblies	
scholarships	seminarians conferences	
DHE	Black Minister's Retreat	
faculty	General Board	
DHM	national student conferences	
student congregations		
field ed personnel		
regional staff		
commissions on ministry		
Post Seminary		
regional staff	General Assembly	
commissions on ministry	regional assemblies	
pastoral relations committees	standing	
	salary	
	continuing education	
	collegiality	
	problem ministries	
	women's and men's groups	

High School and Post High School

As we evaluated the enlistment and under care process of the denomination, it quickly became clear that the process was weak in three areas: 1) lack of coordination between congregations, regions, and general units; 2) lack of a central policy-making body that has responsibility for enlistment for and nurture of ministry; and 3) lack of supervision of the entire process.

Of course, there were other discoveries, and the following list is far from exhaustive:

— Churches are not recruiting as they once did.

— Few materials are written for enlistment.

— Disciple colleges are no longer the primary training ground for seminary studies.

— Costs of schooling are increasing.

— Women are finding placement after seminary difficult.

— National college student conferences have been in decline.

The question which sets this task in motion is, "How do we reach the youth of our congregations in ways that challenge them to give career ministry serious consideration?" To ask the question is an admission of the fact that the church, whether congregation, region, or general unit, has not in recent years targeted our youth as fertile enlistment ground for ministry. Rather than point fingers, the purpose of this work is to offer suggestions on how the church can actively participate in God's call of people to ministry. We are convinced the process is a team effort that includes pastors, parents, congregations, regions, general administrative units of the church, and God.

The obvious place to begin is with those young people who participate in a camp or conference program, youth group, weekend retreat, or, for high school students, the UN Seminar trip. It seems safe to assume that many of the participants in these programs are highly motivated and need to hear a word from the church concerning its leadership needs and the opportunities that are a part of a career in the ministry.

Since regions program most of the youth events beyond local youth groups, it is recommended that a list of participants in these groups be shared with pastors, heads of general units, and with the appropriate regional committees. It is possible to see every gathering of youth as an opportunity for telling the story of ministry.

It would mean that materials would need to be developed by either regions, DHM, DHE, or a combination of all three. Materials could be used on Youth Sunday or during the Week of the Ministry. Every opportunity to talk about the work of ministry should be utilized. Pastors, parents, and lay people are important parts of this process of telling the stories.

Just as congregations need to be intentional in the enlistment process, so does the region. Historically, camps and conferences have been excellent settings for challenging the young people to give serious consideration to the ministry. Most regions have a youth leadership council where this topic could be set before the youth of the region.

Mentors are also important. In addition to parents, pastors, and members of the congregation, the region's staff could play an important role. We should look at the Ohio model that requires regional staff to direct camp and conference. In addition to continuity, the young people have an opportunity to work over several years with the leadership of the region. Youth with the gifts of ministry are identified and can be utilized in leadership roles and in the work of the region.

All of this is but a beginning. The church must walk with, challenge, and model leadership roles for these people from youth long past the time they reach adulthood. The increased average age of students now pursuing first professional degrees in seminaries is indicative of the church's need to nurture and support the decision to enter full-time ministry regardless of the candidate's age.

College and University

A survey was mailed to 100 ministry personnel at Disciples-related colleges and universities and Disciple-related campus ministers at state universities. They were asked to distribute it to Disciples students, and ninety-eight surveys were returned. Approximately 37% came from state universities and 63% from Disciples-related institutions. Thirty-nine percent came from male students and 61% from women. Eighty-four percent came from within the targeted age range of 18-23 years. The returned forms were fairly evenly distributed among years in school, e.g. sophomore, junior. Seventy-two percent of the students responding indicated that they came to school from rural areas, small towns, or small cities.

Ecclesiastical Linkages 27

The remaining 28% came from large cities or the suburbs of large cities. About 44% came from churches of under 200 members. Thirty-five percent came from churches of 200-499 members. The remaining 17% came from churches with 500 to over 1000 members. Three percent were not attending church before they began their undergraduate education.

The goal of the survey was to learn about career decision-making among Disciples undergraduate students, specifically what persons and experiences influenced their decisions. We were interested, also, in whether students might have considered ministry as a career option. And obviously, we were interested in seeing what persons and experiences had influenced those students who had chosen to pursue professional ministry. Of our respondents, 14% had elected ministry as a career, 19% had not yet made a career decision, and 65% had chosen some other career.

In response to the size and denominational affiliation of the church they had attended prior to college, 90% and 94% of the students who had made no career decision or a decision other than ministry (respectively) had come from Disciples backgrounds. In contrast, only 29% of the students who had chosen ministry as a career had come from a Disciples background. Forty-three percent of the students who had chosen ministry as a career had come from denominations more theologically conservative than the Disciples (Assembly of God, Church of Christ, etc.).

Similarly, but not quite as dramatic, were the responses to ways in which students would describe the theological dispositons of their home churches. Thirty-six percent of the students who had chosen ministry as a career indicated that they had come from conservative congregations. Twenty-eight percent of those who had made another career choice, and 16% of those who had not yet made a choice said they had come from conservative congregations.

Results of a question on key events or experiences showed that students who chose ministry as a career were highly influenced by internships, summer jobs, volunteer experiences, and other direct experience with ministry. The percentages were higher than those students who had chosen other professions. Significantly higher (50 compared to 12) was the percentage who said they were influenced by a conference or retreat. We have repeatedly pointed to the influential role of camps, conferences, and other such youth events for enlisting ministerial candidates so that figure confirmed that impression. We also expressed a desire for the reemergence of student movements, both denominational and ecumenical. These results also affirmed our recommendation for better information-sharing and networking of volunteer and paid experiences to give high school and undergraduate students direct experience in ministry.

Pastors were the across-the-board choice when students were asked who they would contact if they were considering ministry as a career. Campus ministers and chaplains ranked second. This confirmed the working assumption that local pastors play a crucial role in the enlistment of ministers. Recommendations related to this observation included adding enlistment as a component of the Week of the Ministry and providing local pastors with more information about seminaries.

Responses to a follow-up question indicated that less than one-half of those students who had chosen another career or had not yet made a choice (42% and 39% respectively) had ever considered ministry as a career. From this we concluded that local churches and youth programs are not highlighting ministry as they once did. When asked why they didn't consider ministry as a career option, students overwhelming responsed that they felt they were not vocationally suited for ministry...their interests and skills were not appropriate for it.

Responding to whether professional ministry had ever been suggested to them, 86% of those who had chosen it answered "yes." Fifty-eight percent of those who had not chosen a career yet answered "no." Fifty-five percent of those who had chosen another career indicated that someone had suggested ministry as an option to them. Local pastors, in all three categories, were most likely to have made the suggestion.

The results of the question on church involvement suggest that, in and of itself, active participation cannot serve as an indicator for students who chose ministry. First, the survey group can be considered to be highly self-selective because it was picked by virtue of students' contact with a chaplain or campus minister. While a higher percentage of those who had chosen ministry as a career (93%) were active in some church organization, 72% of those who had opted for other careers and 84% of those who had yet to decide, were also active in church organizations. The statistics were similar when considering their church involvement before entering college. The variables, therefore, seem to be students' perceptions of their skills, whether ministry is suggested to them, and their perceptions of ministry as a profession.

The written comments in response to the questions about feelings of ministry as a profession and of the role of the church in society make for fascinating reading, although it is difficult to draw conclusions from them. We did get some sense that the students who had chosen ministry as a career had a romanticized vision of ministry and focused almost exclusively on a spiritualized pastoral model, reflecting what seemed to be deficits in sophistication, depth of education, and life experiences.

The demographic information included at the end of the survey also produced some interesting information. While 61% of the total survey responses came from women students, 77% of those indicating that they had chosen ministry as a career were men. Conversely, the gender ratios for those who had chosen another career and those who had yet to make a choice were almost identically reflective of the overall survey gender ratio at 39% male/61% female.

Although not all respondents completed this question, it would seem that a higher percentage of students who have chosen ministry as a career came from Disciples-related institutions. An even higher percentage of those who had yet to make a career decision were from Disciples schools. It is important to remember that the survey went to ALL Disciple-related colleges and universities and only to selected state universities, making the figures unrepresentative.

The age distribution showed that 62% of those who had chosen ministry as a career were in the targeted age range of 18-23 years.

Conclusions

- The congregations in which undergraduate students grew up usually lose touch with them when they leave home to go to school.
- If an undergraduate student is in contact with his/her home and/or campus church, that significantly influences decisions for ministry as a vocational possibility.
- Linkages between congregations that send students to Disciples-related colleges and universities or to any other university, and the church, chaplain, or campus ministry at that institution are weak or nonexistent. This makes the transition from one faith community to another more difficult for a student.
- Hands-on experiences of any type positively impact students' decisions for choosing ministry as a career. There is no formal

system for sharing information about these possibilities with students. They must either search on their own or consult their chaplain or campus minister, who in turn must gather information from a wide variety of sources.

- The home church remains an important point of contact for students in college.
- Regional camps and conferences no longer play the central role in the lives of junior high and high school students they once did.
- If students attend camp or conference, the tradition of making commitments for church vocations is often no longer a part of the experience.
- Disciples-related colleges and universities do not seem to be consistent in viewing Disciples students as candidates for ministerial recruitment.

Recommendations

1. Local churches need to maintain lists of their members in college.

2. Those lists somehow need to be shared with the regional offices, the Division of Higher Education, and the chaplains, campus ministers, and/or local churches at the students' institutions.

3. The church needs to consider using 1 800 NET FIND to link students to chaplains, campus ministers, and/or local churches near the student's college.

4. The denomination needs to support the ongoing development of a national ecumenical student organization and student gatherings (currently Council for Ecumenical Student Ministries).

5. The whole church needs to develop new possibilities for experiences in ministry and find a way to network and publicize existing opportunities. Students connected to the church should have the opportunity to work for the church (Disciples Peace Fellowship internships, National Benevolent Association facilities, summer camps, etc.).

6. Ministry as vocation needs to be presented at college and university Career Fairs. Consider a traveling display that could be staffed by chaplains or campus ministers.

7. The names of all Disciples undergraduate students need to be given to Disciples-related seminaries.

8. Both volunteer and paid opportunities through the church need to be made known to graduating college and university seniors, across disciplines. For example, the Division of Overseas Ministries can advertise possibilities for forestry, agriculture, ESL, etc.

9. Regional committees on the ministry need to develop under care relationships with all potential ministerial candidates of whatever age.

10. More direct links need to be made between local churches and chaplains and campus ministers.

11. Local churches need to be especially aware of the needs and presence of young adults who have graduated from college and whose future is not definite. Consider the Ohio model of Advanced Conference.

12. The church needs to designate a Higher Education Sunday where students can be recognized.

13. In coordination with the Christian Board of Publication, Sunday School curriculum needs to be examined to see if and how it presents ministry as a career option.

Seminary

Based on fall 1989 mailing lists, 379 survey forms were sent to Disciples seminarians with a fifty-seven percent response rate.

The survey questions sought to determine the places where people have contact with various manifestations of the church which might lead them to consider Christian ministry for their life's calling. The survey instrument assumed that an inner relationship between an individual and God was a serious underlying factor. That aspect was not pursued for further information. Some respondents did add that element of their call to ministry, and it was noted on the survey responses. The goal was to identify ways in which, within the church, people are encouraged or nurtured to consider ministry, or have their spiritual calls validated.

It was clear from the responses that the pastor of a congregation plays a significant role in helping people come to a decision for ministry. One-half of the seminarians were directly asked to consider ministry as their profession, and the pastor was the primary person who asked them. When asked to whom -other than family members -the seminarians talked when they were considering ministry as a profession, 79% listed their pastors.

As might be anticipated, a high percentage (88%) of the seminarians were active as young people in their churches, although less than half (47%) of those students were in Disciples churches. Of the seminarians over 25 years of age, 83% were active in their churches since they turned 25, and 60% of those students were in Disciples churches.

When asked what church related events or experiences influenced their choice for ministry, 54% listed volunteer church work and 53% indicated experience in ministry. That percentage may be indicative of a large number of second-career students who may have worked in ministry in some capacity, either volunteer or part time. Thirty-five percent listed conferences and/or retreats as influential.

Students were asked ways in which they had received affirmation for entering ministry. Their possible choices on the survey were people in addition to the church structures closest to an individual such as home church, church they serve, regional office, pastor, and seminary community. The highest response was friends (77%) followed with 73% each for family, home church, and seminary community. Seventy percent said their pastor was supportive, 67% said the "church you serve," and 59% said the regional office. The lowest categories were spouse (50%) and mentor (48%). When asked directly about parents, almost two-thirds said their parents encouraged them, and one-third said they did not.

In terms of direct institutional connections to church agencies which encouraged entry to ministry, 88% of the students said they had never received any contact from a unit of the church about considering ministry. The 11% who had been contacted indicated it was a brochure or letter most likely from a regional office.

After deciding on ministry, candidates found that institutional contact was better established. Eighty-one percent said they had met with their committee (commission) on the ministry, 38% having done so prior to beginning seminary, and 45% during seminary. A majority (60%) met with the committees in their home regions. Thirty-two percent found those meetings very helpful, 40% somewhat helpful, and 11% said such meetings were not helpful. Most seminarians (77%) thought regional ministers ought to meet with ministerial candidates. However, just over half (57%) had met with their regional ministers, and of those 40% had done so at their own request rather than that of the regional ministers. Regardless of whether they had met with a committee on the ministry or with a regional minister, a large majority (85%) said they knew the process for licensing and ordination, and 78% said they had read the *Policies and Criteria for the Order of Ministry*.

When asked what professional person they would talk to first about their future in ministry, 33% said their pastor. The next listed in order were: a professor (19%), their regional minister (18%), their school's field education director (14%), the pastor with whom they work (11%), or the regional minister from the region in which they attend school (10%).

Without question, the local church was most important in preparing students for ministry, according to 81% of the students. Also, 91% were either somewhat (50%) or very (41%) optimistic about the future of the Christian Church (Disciples of Christ), although 75% indicated that their optimism about the church did not affect their choice for ministry as a profession.

When asked to rate the Disciples on a 1 to 10 conservative to liberal scale, students placed the denomination toward the liberal end. Sixty-five percent said the general church is from 7 to 10, and 58% of them placed themselves in that same range. However, they rate only 21% of their home churches at the same point. Sixty-four percent say their home church would rate between 1 and 5 on the conservative end.

Looking at professional goals, the largest single group expects to be associate pastors in the next five years and senior pastors in the next ten years. The majority (75%) anticipate the church structures being helpful in achieving those goals. As far as locations in which they do their ministry, 66% say they want to be in a large city or a suburb of a large city. Also, in looking to the future, almost half (48%) expect an educational debt of $5,000 or less. Twenty-eight percent anticipate an educational debt of $10,000 or more.

Exactly one-half of the students answering the survey were female and one-half male, with 58% married, 32% single, 16% divorced. The average age was 35, and the average age at which they made a decision to enter ministry was 27. The average length of time they had been Disciples was 15.5 years. Twenty percent had been members of the church less than five years, and 39% less than ten years.

The survey asked about students' participation in significant small groups prior to deciding to enroll in seminary. The question was designed to test whether small group involvement and the relationships formed there influence one's thinking about entering ministry. Forty-two percent said a small group, indeed, was influential, and 33% said that it was a church group.

On a related question, 89% said community life with students and faculty outside of class was very important (57%) or somewhat important (32%) in their preparation for ministry.

In addition to ministry, the three professions receiving most consideration were education (41%), social work (26%), and business (35%). Many students had already pursued one of these careers, as 61% are second career students.

Sixty-six percent of the students indicated that they were attending a Disciples affiliated seminary, although a few were not sure if their seminary was officially Disciples-related. Of those at Disciples seminaries, 78% chose it because of the affiliation. The next reason indicated for choice of schools was location (72%), followed by financial aids (30%). Of those not at Disciples institutions, the primary reason for selecting the school was location (71%), followed by academics (58%) and financial aids (32%). When asked what was the most important reason for choosing the school they attended, the students at Disciples schools listed as the top three reasons: financial aid (26%), location (25%), and denominational affiliation (24%). Students at non-Disciples schools listed as most important characteristics: location (34%), academics (14%), and financial aids (6%).

Conclusions

- It is clear that the local pastor and local church are the primary influences in connecting, nurturing, and encouraging people to consider and enter Christian ministry. Also underlying the key role pastors play, was the report that as people thought about ministry, they discussed it with their pastors. When they were in seminary and wanted to talk about their future in ministry many said they would go first to their pastor.

- Church activities, both volunteer and experience in ministry, were highly influential in students becoming interested in ministry. This suggests the importance of strong youth and young adult programs.

- The data seems to support what we probably already knew, that churches with active programs and good pastoral leadership tend to produce candidates for ministry. The minister and the program of the church, both of which engage a person in living out the faith, seem to influence people to consider ministry, or confirm for them the inner "call" which they feel.

- Connections with the other manifestations of the church are few. The main exceptions for some students are conferences, retreats, and exposure to some regional work.
- It would be difficult to pinpoint schools or departments from which to recruit ministerial candidates since the 215 students in this survey represented 141 undergraduate colleges and universities with 76 majors. Those who listed other careers which they had considered noted 45 possibilities. Second career students had been engaged in 64 different vocations before coming to seminary.
- After students are in seminary, the church structures seem to track them well and occasionally offer various kinds of assistance. It was observed, though, that regional ministers generally are not seen as being as helpful as they might be, however, the survey did not try to determine exactly how this might be done.
- Although this project is primarily focused on youth, it would appear that programs of enlistment, for both young adults and second career people, must consider local congregations as the major resource to be addressed.

3

Congregational Enlistment

The purpose of our research was twofold: (1) to profile congregations that have been successful in "producing" quality ministerial candidates, and (2) to profile a selected body of ministers who recall their own enlistment to ministry. The primary focus of our task was to describe the influence of the local congregation in the enlistment of women and men for ordained ministry. In our work, we attempted to develop a representative picture of those congregations which have had notable success in the encouragement and nurture of persons into ministry. We utilized narrative profiles from ordained clergy and seminarians to further enhance our understanding of the factors which influence a person's decision for ministry as well as to serve as a means of verifying the self-reports from congregations. For example, the congregation may have described itself as "encouraging and supportive," but whether clergy and seminarians feel such encouragement and support may be an entirely different evaluation.

We began our work with some ideas, some hunches, and some guesses about what congregations with success in enlisting women and men for ministry might "look like." Some particularly influential factors suggested at the outset of the study by the designers of the grant included the following:

1. The minister serves the congregation over a longer than average period of time and is intentional about modeling ministry for youth.
2. Elders are actively involved as sources of enlistment, nurture, and support for youth.
3. Financial aid is available through congregational scholarship funds for persons choosing to prepare for ministry.
4. An active youth program is present in the congregation.
5. Energetic youth sponsors and able church school teachers provide nurture and support.

In addition to these hypotheses, we wished to inquire about the influence of other dynamics in the local churches which produce ministerial candidates, such as a commitment to camp and conference programs, strength of the entire Christian education program, the importance of lay ministry, the presence of significant outreach ministry, the political/theological stance of the congregation, the adequacy of ministerial compensation, the relationship of the congregation with the regional and general manifestations of the church, and the respect which the congregation has for its professional ministry. The process through which this data was gathered will be described in the next section.

In profiling men and women who were engaged in ordained ministry and those in preparation for ordained ministry, we naturally began with some biases and/or assumptions. One such bias was that for most ordained ministers (or people seeking ordination) the local congregation had been a significant formative factor in their decisions to enter ministry. Even with this prejudice, we still knew that the local church could be both an inhibiting and an encouraging factor. Our survey included only people who did enter ordained ministry, and it is reasonable to assume that people who did not enter ordained ministry might have quite different stories to share about their understandings of the support and nurture of the local congregation. Thus, our survey can represent only those who not only chose ministry but also entered professional ministry, and does not identify those who may have felt God's call but found the walls too high or the barriers too insurmountable. As an example, our work indicates that young white males report a comparatively greater amount of support from the local church. This might be interpreted as an indicator that those who never found enough outward support to sustain their inner call were disproportionately female, people of color, or even gay men or lesbians.

Furthermore, significant questions must be raised regarding the current presumption in church circles which articulate a nostalgic pining for "the golden age" of ministry where quantity in the past is prized while overlooking the quality of ministry in the present. It must be emphasized that even though the Christian Church (Disciples of Christ) faces a certain immediacy in its need for a greater number of qualified ministers, our mission will not be served through a back-handed insult to the presence of highly qualified leaders currently in our congregations.

Additionally, we must caution ourselves as we explore the design of this project and its aim to seek information about young "first career" women and men who enter ministry. The gifts that second career ministers are bringing to the ministry of our church are to be celebrated and affirmed. We must constantly ask whether our concern is with decreasing numbers or with decreasing numbers of young white men. Quite often, as our research progressed, we found the lines between first career ministers and second career ministers blurred in the minds of nurturing congregations and even in the minds of minister themselves. We must ask the question, "Is the differentiation fair or even necessary?"

As our exploration progressed, several obstacles were met. Initially we were faced with a problem perhaps molded around our peculiar nature as the Christian Church (Disciples of Christ). As a decentralized people, there is no "magical place" where a list of congregations that have produced/enlisted/ discerned women and men for ministry is kept. We attempted to uncover this information through the existing structures. However, we found that access to some structures was limited by our lack of understanding of the structures themselves! A related complicating factor was the frustrating fact that once we uncovered possible congregations to be interviewed, many of them did not have complete or adequate records in their own files to answer all of the questions.

Throughout our process we were intentionally inclusive. Yet, somehow, not inclusive enough. Our work does not adequately represent the richness of our diversity as a denomination. Specifically, the Black, Hispanic, and Asian-American experience is not effectively explored. [Editor's note: Further study to address the experience of the Convocation, the Assembly Churches, the Hispanic Convention, and the Asian-American churches is contained in Chapter Five of this volume.]

Understandably, the accuracy of the data gathered in profiling local congregations was difficult to assess. Through surveys and interviews we asked respondents to reflect on the past and the present. Oftentimes these may have melded together in the respondent's mind. Furthermore, one must ask how one distinguishes between myth and reality. Is our memory always as accurate as we imagine it to be? The memory of a congregation may not reflect the way "it" actually was. For example, three or four congregations would claim the same person as a "Priscilla" or "Timothy," each believing there was a substantial reason to do so. In addition, congregational memory borders at times on being more of an indicator of "how we wish it could be today..." rather than as a strictly historical account. As one team member put it, "How does the church of the past reflect on the future?"

Finally, we raised concerns regarding the question of retention/ attrition in ministry. The way in which the church nurtures people after the decision for ordained ministry is as crucial in the discussion of quality ministers as is the concern about their enlistment.

Procedures

We began the process of locating the congregations that had been "successful" in enlisting persons into the ministry by sending a form in July 1989 to 35 regional ministers requesting the names of congregations known for producing ministerial candidates. (Which immediately raised the concern that the "quality" of a church's success may or may not be legitimately defined by the "quantity" of persons who have entered ministry from that congregation.) Follow-up calls were made and forms were received from 27 regions. The 100 plus congregations identified by regional ministers, in addition to those congregations named by team members in order to provide a broader representation of persons, each received a survey and letter in late August asking for the following: names of "Priscillas/Timothies," their ages at time of ordination, and the name and tenure of the pastor or pastors serving the congregation at time of ordination; the nature of financial aids provided by the congregation; the presence and strength of the church's youth program; other factors they considered that encouraged people about ministry; and demographic data (size, racial make-up, location). Eighty-five completed surveys were returned by the congregations contacted. Of this group, forty were selected for phone interviews by team members (eight congregations with minority constituencies, 32 with white constituencies.) Advance letters were sent to those forty congregations explaining that they would be contacted for an interview during February 1990. Letters were sent to the senior pastor except in cases where another contact had already been established through earlier correspondence.

The phone interviews consisted of 28 questions grouped in the following areas: general data about the congregation and "Timothies/Priscillas," ministerial scholarships, children and youth programming, nature of relationship between congregation and pastor (including tenure, salaries, level of respect, and compensation), and other factors (derived particularly from the results of previous surveys) including such areas as support of lay ministry, outreach ministry, political/theological stance of congregation, relationship with Disciples colleges and seminaries, relationship with missionaries, and relationship with general/regional structures. Thirty interviews were conducted. Four of these congregations were predominately Black, two described themselves as racially mixed, and one congregation was predominately Hispanic.

In profiling a selected body of women and men who recall their own enlistment to ministry, our team generated a list of 135 "quality" clergy and 40 "quality" seminarians. "Quality" is difficult to define and measure. Our team understood quality as a term which encompasses genuiness, integrity, commitment, creativity, and the evidence of fruitfulness in the person's ministry. The list generated was an attempt to reflect the diversity of our denomination. Of the 138 initial profiles mailed to ordained ministers, 40 were sent to people of color. Forty-eight were women; ninety were men. Our team sought to include people in all forms of ministry. The initial "quality" seminarian profiles were sent to persons whose names were obtained from seminary presidents, registrars, and alumni. Approximately ten additional profiles were sent to seminarians of African-American or Hispanic origin whose names were recommended following the initial mailing. Eighty-seven profiles were received from ordained clergy. Of that number 59 were male, 27 female (one no response), 63 were Caucasian, 21 African-American, two Hispanic, one Asian. Twenty-eight profiles were received from seminarians. Of that number 15 were female, 13 male; 20 were Caucasian, seven African-American, one Hispanic.

The survey tool that was developed asked for narrative responses to twelve questions in the following areas: formative influences inside/outside the church that led to a decision for ministry; nature of calling; perception of ministry as an esteemed profession; formalized training received; structures of church that provided nurture; perceptions of reasons colleagues leave ministry; and demographic data (age at time of decision for ministry, age and year of ordination, size of "home" church, gender, ethnic background, current form of ministry.)

Findings

In surveying both the individual churches selected for their success in the recruitment of persons into ministry and quality ordained ministers and seminarians, we found the variety of responses both exciting and challenging. Each person surveyed gave a different emphasis to questions. Occasionally the congregational representative who was involved in a phone interview would be one of the ministers who had sent in information as a "quality minister." One church official surveyed would find an element extremely important, while another might not even mention it. The overall

42 *Discerning the Call*

result is more of a mosaic of factors gleaned from churches and quality ministers than a detailed account of "what ought to be done."

The structure of each section following is based on the questions asked in the phone interviews with churches. Thirty phone surveys were completed, although not all questions were answered by each respondent. Information received from the profiling of quality ministers and seminarians serve as the means to "flesh out" the church interviews.

Initially congregations were asked to provide the names and years of persons enlisted into ministry. Twenty-six congregations responded with a total of 212 persons entering the ministry which averages eight persons per congregation. Nineteen of the congregations reported that the primary period of recruitment occurred from 1960 to the present. In general this mirrors the group of clergy surveyed, the majority of whom were ordained since 1960. The congregations responding ranged in size from a low of 100 active participants to a high of 2,500 active participants. The average size church in this study was approximately 600 active members (500 not counting the two congregations above 500), well above the average size congregation in the Christian Church (Disciples of Christ).

Scholarships

Of the thirty congregations surveyed, all but two have a scholarship program. Of those that do, twenty are in the form of an outright gift, three are in the form of a loan. Eight of the scholarship programs specified monies for undergraduate studies, and 24 earmarked monies for seminary or ministerial training. The dollar amounts varied from a low of $50 per semester to a high of $1,000 per semester with seven congregations reporting that the dollar amounts were determined on a need basis. Twelve of the scholarship programs were funded through endowments, trusts, or memorial gifts. Twelve were budgeted items. Special offerings accounted for four of the scholarship grants. Christian Womens' Fellowships were responsible in two instances. One congregation did not provide a scholarship fund though it did contribute regularly to the Star Supporter Fund.[22]

Though there were several instances in which congregations provided scholarships for both undergraduate and seminary students, such as University Christian Church in San Diego, California and First Christian Church of Corpus Christi, Texas most of the funds were available primarily for those in seminary or, more generally, those going into "ministerial training."

One example of an intentional attempt at funding ministerial scholarships is First Christian Church in Martinsville, Indiana. Ten percent of its recent capital campaign was designated for a scholarship program for persons seeking a Master of Divinity degree. The invested fund amounts to approximately $15,000. Bethany Christian Church in Ft. Washington, Maryland uses the interest from a substantial trust fund to provide scholarships for persons who can verify they are headed toward seminary training, regardless of whether they are members of the Bethany church. Additional grants go directly to Disciples-related seminaries from this fund.

Overall, the congregations surveyed reported that the presence of a scholarship fund was known by those members of the congregations who might be interested. However, we did not find such scholarships to be used as an overt means of encouraging young people to consider the ministry as a career, nor were they extensively publicized. Park Avenue Christian Church in Des Moines, Iowa intentionally sends scholarship forms to those students who are know to be eligible, but the fund is not "advertised" per se. Several of those responding from congregations commented that they believed scholarship monies were not so much responsible for encouraging persons to go into the ministry as they were meaningful in undergirding and supporting persons once they began their training.

Children and Youth Programming

As other surveys such as the May 1989 "Study of the Quality in the Ministry of the Christian Church (Disciples of Christ)"[23] have shown, the presence of a strong local church experience during childhood and adolescence plays a formative role in the decision for ministry. In our survey of congregations, the majority of the 28 congregations answering this question reported that their congregation maintains a good educational program. Twenty-five felt that the Sunday School was strong, seventeen commented on strength in the Chi Rho and CYF programs, and seventeen felt the camp and conference programs were meaningful. Reflecting on the past, these congregations reported a history of strong programming for children and youth. For example, out of 27 responses, 24 reported a strong Sunday School program, 24 for Chi Rho and CYF, and 22 for camp and conference.

While recognizing the lower numbers in current programs, several of those interviewed acknowledged that mere numbers were not the sole indication of success and believed that current programming might simply fill a different need in society and in the church. Robert

Sulanke, retired minister of Hazlewood Christian Church in Muncie, Indiana, commented that the Sunday School at Hazlewood is still a good program; it is just a different program than before.

The importance of children and youth programming was supported by our profile of quality ministers and seminarians. Over half of the respondents, both in the ministerial and the seminarian groups, listed a local youth program as an important early church activity. We note that the percentages here were much greater for Caucasian respondents than for any other group.

Our surveys also indicated that camps and conferences were seen as crucial nurturers of an interest in ministry as fifteen churches stressed these as formative events. Churches such as First Christian in Baxter Springs, Kansas and First Christian in Martinsville, Indiana continue to send youth to camp in outstanding numbers. Several ordained ministers noted participation in camps and conferences as influential factors in their decisions to enter ministry, and about fifty percent of the ministers surveyed, fewer African-American males than others, mentioned their participation in camps and conferences as being important church activities.

Other factors that were listed by ministers and seminarians as influential included such things as area and regional youth programming, music and choir involvement, Vacation Church School, and participation in worship.

Twenty-four of the responding churches cited "Timothies/ Priscillas" as being involved in youth programs, of which 22 remembered them as leaders. In addition, these congregations provided opportunities for leadership in non-youth related areas, and youth often accepted these roles. Seventeen churches cited youth as having representation on functional committees, sixteen had youth either in the regular diaconal structure or in a junior diaconate, and nineteen had youth involved in handbell or voice choirs. Park Avenue Christian Church in Des Moines, Iowa had an extensive youth music ministry during the 1970s and early 1980s, the same time period when approximately six persons from that church were ordained into Christian ministry. While a direct correlation between this activity and the number of ordinations is impossible to make, the youth music program was unquestionably successful in involving large numbers of youth and is still remembered as a vital period of youth ministry in that congregation.

Many of these congregations encouraged youth to gain a broader understanding of "the Church," by providing opportunities for youth to participate in area/district, regional, and general events. This primarily, but not exclusively, took the shape of camp and conference involvement. Likewise, these congregations provided experiences in which youth encountered the social dimensions of the gospel through both service and community-building. Twenty-four of the congregations cited youth trips as one facet of their youth programs. The frequency, intensity, and nature of youth trips varied greatly from congregation to congregation. Several congregations mentioned work projects such as "Habitat for Humanity," choir tours for witness and fun, bell choir tours, Disciples Heritage tours, and entertainment activities such as ski trips. The youth of First Christian Church of Frankfort, Kentucky have made regular trips to a variety of places, including a work trip to Jamaica and fun/educational trips to the Disciples of Christ Historical Society, Cane Ridge, and Transylvania University. Regional youth events such as the "Models for Ministry" event sponsored by Chapman College and the Christian Youth Fellowship in the Southwest Assembly at Texas Christian University were also mentioned.

Nature of Relationship between Congregation and Pastor

Along with a strong educational emphasis, congregations cited the presence of professional and lay leadership in Christian education and youth programming as a significant factor in the health of their churches. Twenty-two congregations had paid staff involved in youth programming with 25 indicating significant lay involvement.

Again, these findings were supported in our profile of ordained clergy and seminarians. The majority of seminarians listed minister and youth minister along with family as important role models. Clergy, too, found pastoral and youth ministers to be key role models, and women noted especially the importance of female role models.

The average length of the senior minister's tenure during the primary period of recruitment to ministry was sixteen years. The average tenure of the minister currently serving each the congregations was reported as eight years. Highland Park Christian Church in Des Moines, Iowa has had only three ministers in the past sixty years and at least eight persons entered ordained ministry during that same time period.

When asked how they would describe the congregation's respect for ministry, all of the congregations gave positive responses. One team member, as an example, interviewed seven congregations. Of those, six responded to the question "How would you describe the congregation's respect for ministry?" with two words: "Very High." Others elaborated on their response with comments such as: "We respect the minister's opinions." "There's a certain confidence bestowed in the minister." "The minister is dearly loved and respected." and "Yes, we take the minister seriously."

Related to this question of respect for the minister is the role ministers play in influencing persons to consider ministry as a vocation. In profiling ordained ministers, a strong percentage of persons, less so for Caucasian females, saw a pastor as an influential factor in being led to consider Christian ministry.

In an attempt to build an objective picture of the congregation's relationship with the pastor, the following specific questions were asked and are listed along with the responses: The presence of a pastoral relations committee -18 yes, 10 no. A Minister's "Hall of Fame" (i.e. gallery of previous ministers' pictures) -14 yes, 13 no. Timothy/Priscilla "Hall of Fame" -8 yes, 16 no.

To further understand the pastor/parish relationship, information about compensation was sought. Sixteen of the 20 congregations who provided dollar amounts reported a salary and housing package of over $31,000 for the senior minister. Twelve of those were over $41,000. Three described their salary as "adequate," one as "attractive," and one as "inadequate." The majority of respondents include a social security offset, continuing education expenses, and conference and assembly expenses as well as the almost universal pension payments as part of the benefit package.

In much the same way, lay ministry is also emphasized and supported by these congregations. Twenty-three churches agreed that lay ministry was an important part of the congregation's leadership. Several times those interviewed stated that the clergy often provided the impetus or the direction for ministry, but that it was the laity that actually did much of the work. Especially important for lay ministry was the area of visitation such as hospital and homebound. One minister said that the congregation he pastors has a strong history of "saints" in the congregation. Laity Sunday was a vehicle for several churches to highlight and implement a more intentional lay ministry.

Evangelical Church Disciples of Christ in the Bronx, New York has a tremendous amount of lay involvement in several substantial areas of church life. Members lead worship services in individual homes as well as at the church, where lay men and women may also preach. This community leadership is balanced by the deep sense of respect members of the Evangelical Church have for their minister.

Other Avenues in Which Congregations Would Be Exposed to Ordained Ministry

We were interested in the influence that institutions of higher education might have in highlighting ministry as vocation, especially if there is a significant relationship between Disciples seminaries and universities and a local congregations. Nineteen of 27 congregations reported some form of relationship with such an institution. The relationships varied and included interaction such as youth attending Disciples-related colleges and universities following graduation, participation of a church in the regional support system of a seminary, youth trips to Disciples colleges and seminaries, the utilization of speakers and preachers from various colleges and seminaries, college-sponsored CYF days, connections through an institution's fund-raising efforts, and interns from Disciples colleges and seminaries. While these results show that there are several means of contact between local congregations and Disciples institutions of higher education, interviews often confirmed that these contacts were in many cases tentative and lacked cultivation.

We were interested in the presence and impact of ministerial internship positions in local congregations. Sixteen congregations had previously employed or presently have seminarians as interns. In addition, eleven had provided internships for college students, and three reported some form of high school internship program. Four congregations have participated in the STEEM program.[24] The internships covered a variety of formats. One church encourages high school youth to "shadow" the minister in order to experience the work of a pastor. Vine Street Christian Church in Nashville, Tennessee has had 60 to 65 people in its paid intern program since 1965, and the current minister of this church was an intern himself in the Vine Street congregation. University Christian Church in San Diego, California reports a steady stream of interns from the School of Theology at Claremont, many of these often choose to celebrate their ordination at University Church because of their enriching experience there. First Christian Church of Frankfort, Kentucky participates in a District-wide "Summer Ministerial Apprenticeship" program which involves a person considering ministry as a career in a ten-week experiential program as well as education about ministry. This includes assistance with worship services, hospital visitation, seminars with pastors, and attendance of classes at Lexington Theological Seminary.

Our profiles of ordained ministers and seminarians supported the idea that involvement in the church in an intentional and educational way was helpful in strengthening their interest in ministry. The importance of having a respected minister or authority in one's life who specifically encourages one to go into ministry was cited. In evaluating the training they received for ministry, some respondents affirmed that their "field experience was encouraging" and that "practical training was priceless" while others said there was too little practical help. Several ministers specified that it was not so much a "home" congregation that nurtured their interest in ministry, but rather their field placement or seminary church that did so. Some seminarians, in the midst of statements which indicate strong appreciation for their seminary training, criticized their education for lacking enough application to the "real life tasks of ministry," and several noted specific items such as direction on church financing and congregational board structures as being missing elements in their education.

The team was also interested in the exposure of members of the congregation, especially children and youth, to other ministers in the community and the wider church structure. For instance, we explored whether congregations enjoy a strong connection with a missionary or with a campus minister. Seventeen congregations noted some contact with non-parish ministry. Responses varied and included the visit of fraternal workers to the congregation, participation in the former "Living Link" missionary program, the work of a "Priscilla" in the social services field, and a pastor's wife working in mission churches. Others highlighted the use of the church building by a variety of groups which broadens the congregation's awareness of various types of ministries. An additional means of exposure to other ministries was seen through the regional manifestation of the church. Some youth experience mission work first-hand by actually participating in on-site mission work, whether through a special travel opportunity or through regular weekly events.

Outreach and Social Action Ministries

Many of the surveyed congregations saw their own outreach and social action ministry as an important extension of the congregation itself. Twenty-five stressed a strong outreach, social action, or mission ministry. Again, several churches understood the utilization of their building by community service groups as a very real means of ministering to the community. National City Christian Church in Washington D.C. houses a school for emotionally disturbed children, a day school, a thrift shop, an international craft shop, and meeting spaces and offices for numerous community organizations. A significant number of churches that responded were involved in their community either through food banks, local ecumenical work, pastoral counseling centers, or simply through the volunteer hours that church members give to community organizations. Some churches minister to the community through advocacy and support of social issues. First Christian Church in Tuscon, Arizona is involved in the issue of peace, the Sanctuary movement, and advocacy for the homeless. Highland Park Christian Church in Des Moines, Iowa has been involved in preventing the closure of an inner-city high school, in fighting for housing for the elderly, and in supporting the building of a new public library.

The profiled ministers frequently concurred with the importance of outreach and social ministries in the Christian life. In response to the question regarding activities beyond the church being formative for persons entering ministry, regular references were made to outreach and social ministries. Such activities and influences include working in the Civil Rights Movement; the needs of the poor and others in the world; being a camp director for troubled youth; the challenge of faith and justice issues; work with deaf children; a mother involved in education and politics; college work with peace and social justice issues; the problems of war, poverty, racism, and sexism; and the need to share good news with one's community.

Conclusions

The work done by the members of this committee is valuable primarily if seen as a "picture" or a "mosaic" of churches that have had unusual success in the enlistment of persons into the ministry rather than as a "documentation" of what is and what ought to be. There were several meaningful insights and compelling recommendations that team members gleaned from these "pictures." The profiles of quality ordained ministers and of quality seminarians served as an important means of cross-checking our recommendations.

1. Intentionality

One of the most pervasive needs in this whole process of nurture, encouragement, advocacy, and support for persons interested in the ministry as a career is the basic need for intentionality. Successful churches were those where scholarship programs were intentionally funded and managed, where ministers were intentional about being role models and about suggesting to qualified young people the possibility of a career in ministry, where internship programs were well thought out, and where the involvement of youth in the on-going life of the church was intentional, no matter how many youth were present.

2. Clergy Models

An almost universal affirmation of the importance of the individual minister in modeling a caring and committed approach to ministry was found. Many ordained ministers noted particular pastors, some from their home churches and some from their field education experiences, who had provided a healthy example of ministry as a compelling and rewarding career. Conversely, women and racial/ethnic minorities often lamented the lack of role models that were also women and racial/ethnic minorities.

3. Opportunities for Youth to Minister

While there was little agreement on the exact form it should take, there was considerable consensus amongst surveyed churches that youth ought to be involved in ministry. Though the traditional youth programming continues, many other means of involving youth, not just in activities but in ministry itself, are taking place. Youth are taking mission trips to help others, youth are leading worship and doing hospital ministry, youth are presenting choir concerts, and they are serving communion. In short, youth find ministry compelling when they are given the opportunity actually to be immersed in ministry.

4. Engagement in Real Life

Frequently, those ministers and seminarians questioned about their training reported they were unprepared for ministry in the real world. If young people grow up in churches where there are long pastorates and a generally healthy respect for ministry, they may be surprised that such an attitude is not more prevalent throughout the church. Intentional, well-structured, and fully-supported internships for college and seminary students is a necessary means of connecting the ideals and hopes for ministry with the reality of ministry. A side effect that is not to be overlooked is the importance of role modeling by these interns on interested young people in the congregation. The more models of ministry there are in a single congregation, the greater are the chances that a young person will be "turned on" by ministry.

5. Support

The visible support of ministers from the time candidates leave a local church to go to college until beyond their retirement is inestimable in the encouragement of persons for ministry. While we found little correlation between scholarships programs and the initial interest in ministry, we did find constant evidence that the retention of students in seminaries, and the health and happiness of ministers in ministerial settings, were related to the extent to which they were supported emotionally, spiritually, and financially.

6. Understanding Calling as a Process

The concept of the call into ministry as a gradual process must be further explored and developed within congregational settings. While some people may receive a call to ministry through a sudden life-changing moment, many more reported that they were "nuturerd" into ministry over a period of years. A common perception of call may be similar to that of Paul's conversion as recorded in Acts, yet this can discourage young people from recognizing and acting on God's subtle tugging and gradual leading. Ordained ministers, seminarians, and church officers all verbalized that on-going relationships in the life of the church were important to their understanding of the call to ministry.

7. Respect for Ministry

The respect that successful churches have for their ministers can be seen in concrete ways in the church and, significantly, the results were similarly concrete: there was an overwhelming correlation between long pastorates and churches that had been successful in the enlistment of people into ministry. Churches must continue to recognize and demonstrate their responsibilities to care for ministers and to celebrate and affirm the gifts and graces of persons in ministry.

4

Faith Development

The portion of the overall project which we were asked to address, *adolescent development and the role of faith in that development*, proved to be a complex issue. Our struggle with the nature of our assignment gave rise to questions which we felt compelled to engage as a preface to our report.

1. Our first difficulty stemmed from the wording of the assignment "...to identify faith development in adolescents *in order to understand appropriate times, ways, and means to approach youth and young adults with the career option of ministry*" (emphasis ours). There is danger of becoming absorbed in a quest for increasing numbers and ignoring the need to improve the overall quality of ministry and mission.

What is the real nature of the crisis which faces the church today? Does the crisis lie in a diminished number of ministerial candidates? Or, does it lie in a diminished sense of what it means to be the church in the modern milieu? Are we losing "quality" young people because we have already lost ways in which faithfully to initiate persons into a self-identity and way of life that is decisively different from the dominant culture?

Perhaps when the church is sufficiently engaged in who God is and what God does in the world, the problem of declining ministerial leadership will cease to exist. In that case, the church would continue to participate in mediating a call to ministry by discerning those gifts and graces that the church needs for its leadership in a particular time, place, and circumstance, and would be free of concern for numbers.

2. Is there a "ministerial typology" sufficient for the needs of the church? Ministry is identified too readily with the professional ordained clergy. Since Schleiermacher, the "clergy paradigm" has dominated Protestant views of ministry. If the church is to remain a vital presence in the rapidly changing world, it cannot hang onto

models that have hypostasized ministry into the solitary form of the pastor tending "his" flock (and, regrettably, the male pronoun still seems to be the norm in the minds of many church persons). We find this paradigm too hierarchical, too authoritarian, too static, and too disabling to the vital ministry of the total congregation to remain the paradigm of ministry. In its place, we propose a congregationally based, shared approach to ministry. The "congregational paradigm," in which ministry proceeds dialogically, under the leadership of "set apart" clergy, is more appropriate to the needs of the church today and tomorrow.[25]

The clergy paradigm presents another problem. The present clergy (and their extensions in the institutions of the denomination) have historically been the agents of the "call" extended to "candidates" for ministry. This has tended to result in a succession of clergy with similar views of the church, world, theology, persons, and so forth. In other words, the present crisis in the ministry seems to reflect an "old boys" network in which current clergy "tap" persons as candidates for ministry who are similar to themselves. While an overstatement, it is not far from the truth to claim that the generation of clergy following those now reaching retirement age wear the same suits, have the same haircuts, the same theological training, and the same orientation toward the church and its mission. The church would benefit from a wider variety of personality types, a wider racial/ethnic distribution, and more women in the pulpit than the "old boys" network has been willing to allow.

3. We prefer to speak of the "call to vocation" in its various forms, rather than addressing the nature of ministry as a "career" or a "profession." These latter terms stress human initiative as opposed to God's call and response to it, and the care and connectedness to community that response evokes. The terms "career" and "profession" also point toward technical training rather than theological education and spiritual formation.

A distinctly theological frame of reference needs to be recognized and communicated rather than attempting to "package the ministry" to make it a more attractive profession to young people today. The church needs firstly to emphasize the call to vocation and ministry mediated to every Christian in their baptism. This means we must help each Christian articulate vocational questions: Who is God, and what does God want of my life? How can my own enjoyments, skills, and gifts best be used to participate in God's work in the world? A lively sense of the vocation of all baptized Christians will mitigate perpetuation of the clergy paradigm.

We must not domesticate the call to ministry, lay or ordained. We need a more "Spirit popping" frame of reference! Discerning ways in which to live out one's Christian vocation is often a messy process. The church needs to learn and practice ways in which to participate with persons in mystery, messiness, struggle, paradox, or ambiguity.

One theological tension that obviously exists for the church is between maintaining its responsibility to set aside its leadership, and recognizing that in God's provisions for the church, sometimes God surprisingly calls persons whom the church might otherwise overlook.

Another theological tension appears when we understand that the church needs strong, articulate, and decisive leaders while it also needs to re-order itself according to a congregational rather than a clergy paradigm for ministry.

4. What is adolescence? The assignment seemed to assume that the target group for our work is adolescents understood by chronological age. This was troublesome because all of us became aware of our "calls" during college years or later. We suspect our experiences may be more the norm than the exception.

Moreover, adolescence, as a strictly developmental rather than age-correlated phenomenon, means that the developmental leaps expected to occur during adolescence might not take place until an individual's late twenties or even early thirties. Yet that age bracket is well beyond the ages of 14-22 as indicated in the assignment. The developmental leaps marking the transition from adolescence to young adulthood are occurring much later for vast numbers of young people in contemporary culture. Many young persons delay career choices and also shift career plans in their early postgraduate years.

The church cannot abstract young people from their powerful sub-cultural milieu and still expect to have an effective ministry with them. Is the church ready for the changes that might result in the ways we define ministry and the ways we experience the church if we take seriously the contributions of the contemporary youth culture?

What then is the nature of the developmental age group we are considering? We offer some suggestions toward a fresh appraisal of young persons, the contributions they might make to the work of the church and its mission in the world, and their potential for the call to ministry.

Theological Issues in the Church's Ministry with Youth

Consideration of the special call to ordained Christian ministry must be preceeded by the question of the general call to become a Christian. In turn, the general call is understood as God's reconciling and steadfast love bringing persons into covenantal relationship with God and with all persons. The Christian community is the embodiment of that Story and Vision in, with, and for the world. It is a covenantal community engaged in witness and mission.

Using Niebuhr's typology in *Christ and Culture*,[26] we rejected the Christ *against* culture, Christ *of* culture, Christ and culture *in paradox*, and Christ *above* culture options, and affirmed Christ *transforming* culture. We understand this to include not only the role of transforming culture with its systems and institutions but also persons. Niebuhr's emphasis on the theme of dialogue and I-thou relationships is shared by the group, and appears in many forms in this chapter.

We are convinced that *presence* with youth in their culture, and youth's experience in the adult culture (with its systems, both sinful and good), are important aspects of ministry and mission. Both youth culture and adult culture are ambiguous, however, and need critical reflection in terms of the Gospel Story and Vision (Thomas Groome). There are, of course, various understandings of the content of the Story.

There was consensus among us that life is best understood in terms of a lifelong journey. An important way to understand the journey is through developmental theory, although each of us may employ developmental theories in diverse ways.

Methodology

We began by telling our own life stories, identifying the influences, persons, and events related to our developmental journeys that brought us ("called" us) into the ordained ministry. In addition, each of us drew upon experiences of ministry with youth, as well as upon theoretical and empirical studies we had integrated into our approaches to youth ministry. We considered ways in which our own background experience both illumined and raised questions about our assigned task.

Two main trends in youth ministry emerged: a *youth-cultural* emphasis and a *developmental* emphasis. While overlapping, they differ in significant ways. The youth-cultural approach sees knowledge of, and participation in, youth sub-culture, especially as carried by music, as the *sine qua non* of relating and being present with youth. The developmental approach also considers participation in culture as important, but rather than the youth sub-culture, gives emphasis to the adult work culture and marginalized cultures. It employs awareness of the stages of development (Erikson and Fowler and variations of both) as helpful in identifying tasks and experiences important to a young person's journey.

If youth culture and adult culture are seen as two interrelated poles, youth ministry is a matter of keeping attention to the two poles balanced and inter-actional (over against a hierarchical relationship between them). While they both affirm to-and-fro dialogue between the two cultures, the *youth-cultural* and *developmental* approaches give relative emphasis in one direction or another. In the former, emphasis is placed on adults moving into youth culture, becoming familiar with it, and helping youth critically reflect on it. In the latter approach, emphasis is given to involving and initiating youth into the wider adult culture, particularly as a means of helping them achieve identity-formation, the major developmental task of adolescence. Whereas the developmental emphasis brings a strong "hermeneutic of suspicion" to youth culture and culture at large, the youth-cultural emphasis is much more optimistic about the sub-cultural contributions to the quest for meaning and maturity.

The Youth-Cultural Emphasis

Most pastors and parents find high schoolers baffling. And this is for good reason. Our society, quite without intending it, has produced a distinct youth culture which strongly influences teenagers' behavior. This culture is ever-changing, and its music, clothing styles, and "in" expressions shift from year to year.[27]

Considering ordained ministry and youth culture in the same breath appears to be an exercise of putting square pegs in round holes. The silly non-conformity, permissiveness, and whims of youth appear to have little to do with the life and death importance, responsibility, and mystery of ordained ministry.

In many ways, there is little in common between the interests of youth culture and those of ordained ministry. Yet, in some respects, they share related values. The youth culture (more accurately, the youth sub-culture) rebels against the dominant culture. It is marginal to, yet immersed in society, giving it potential for the transformation of that society.

58   *Discerning the Call*

Youth, along with the church, long for a sense of immediacy in life experience, especially of the Transcendent. Youth culture is open to the Transcendent, to God to come "popping into life." Seemingly trivial moments carry the possibility of the religiously significant. These create the stories and symbols of life through which youth can participate in the larger culture and in a sacred story. The assumption that youth sub-culture is merely a God-forsaken, foreign land is to be challenged. Within their culture, youth constantly seek for meaning. They search through story-telling, pop music, art, cinema, and other symbolic expressions. They "mine for grace" in the sub-cultural terrain. Such mining is both constructive and destructive; it can lead youth to either cosmos or chaos. Sometimes youth "look for love in all the wrong places."

One observer of culture states, "We need to ask ourselves why our culture is bereft of meaningful stories and images that young adults turn to rock music in order to experience transcendence."[28] In fact, our culture is not bereft of meaningful stories and images; some of them are reflected in the youth sub-culture.

Youth culture relies on popular music as its primary mediator. In it are found credo and confession, hope and despair, discovery and loss, reality and legend, sham and symbol.

> The function of popular music has not received much notice from sociologists, who perversely have spent more time assessing the impact of television despite the fact that many people from the ages of ten to twenty-five are more heavily exposed to radio and records. For many people in this age group, popular music provides a *sense of change*, as records and styles replace each other in that instant history of the hit parades. *At any time in this history, each listener has a few records that enrich his (her) feelings, extend his (her) sense of life or despair*, and feed his (her) fantasies or fire some real relationship. He (she) switches on the radio and waits for this music, or buys the records and plans his (her) own program of moods [emphasis ours].[29]

One feature of rock music in the 1980s is its involvement with social causes. Most notable were the large fund raising efforts: Live Aid, Farm Aid, and Band Aid. Different issues and concerns are often mediated in songs, albums, benefit concerts, and exhibits at concerts. Examples include: Campus Outreach Opportunity League (10,000 Maniacs), South Africa (Artists United Against Apartheid—the Sun City Project)), Greenpeace (REM, Public Image, Ltd., Grateful Dead),

Friends of Amnesty International (a five-continent tour with Tracy Chapman, Bruce Springsteen, Sting, and Peter Gabriel).

Film, fashion, television, music videos (MTV), theatre, dance, art, and literature are also included within youth sub-culture. "Miami Vice" utilized rock music and rock performers as actors. Indeed, a whole manner of dress grew out of that show. In the past, psychedelic music, closely identified with the "hippie movement," created and expressed whole philosophies, some of which are insightful and revelatory, some destructive, but all respond to the desire for life, not death.

"Punk" found its primary expression through the band, The Sex Pistols. Their influence was expressed by clothing and jewelry (torn, ragged, safety pins), theatre, and art. Greil Marcus, a cultural commentator, compares the punks with several philosophical and artistic movements whose effect on the broader culture far exceeds their initial influence.[30]

A growing phenomenon, "World Beat," portrays the inclusion of musical styles from other cultures. The best example is Jamaican reggae music. However, other cultures are also successful in North America, such as: South African folk music (due to Paul Simon's efforts) and Spanish folk music (The Gipsy Kings). Another example is rap music. Long present within the urban Black street culture, it has significantly altered North American popular music. In addition, the dance, art, and fashions of rap are now being felt within the broader culture. Through this exchange of popular music, a global youth sub-culture is emerging.

The all-encompassing nature of the youth sub-culture suggests parallels to religion. Religion is a culture into which persons must be initiated, as such, it influences values, moods, thoughts, sentiments, and overall ways of doing and being in the world. Youth sub-culture has the same effect! It functions as a whole, with each aspect affecting and conditioning the other. What occurs in music finds expression in art and fashion and dance and so on.

Youth culture seems remote, foreign, and unstable. But it must be considered in understanding young people and "recruiting" them for ordained ministry. Youth culture includes experience, both good and bad, that informs the spiritual quest of youth. "Popular culture provides an opportunity to experience God and to tell stories of God or...to learn about God and to teach about God."[31] We know so little of youth culture that we are unable to see any "burning bush" there. Furthermore, there apears to be little desire to seriously become involved with youth culture. Only by believing that hope, meaning, and grace can be mediated within youth culture, can we enter and be present to youth where they dwell. One approach to being present with youth in their culture is suggested below.

A Dialogical Approach

There are several things to understand about true dialogue. First, true dialogue avoids a hierarchical relationship, described as an "I-it" relationship. This happens when one person regards the other as an object, as a means to an end. One person "tells" another, speaks to rather than with another, and essentially engages in a monologue.

An alternative to an "I-it" relationship is an "I-thou" relationship, in which the other is regarded as a fellow subject, deserving equal consideration in the conversation. However, one may respect another without allowing that person to have an effect on one's own perspective. Instead of dialogue, that is a two-person monologue; neither party is affected by the claim to truth of the other.

A true "I-thou" relationship not only acknowledges the essential worth of the other person, but also allows that person to challenge one's view of the world. When monologue gives way to dialogue, one becomes vulnerable, and acknowledges one's limited perspective on "truth." True dialogue changes the partners who engage in conversation, and calls them to change the world with which they interact.

This suggests that we refocus our ministry with youth, engaging them as partners in *dialogue*, rather than recipients of adult learned *monologues*. Instead of expecting youth to become like us, adults need to encourage and initiate interaction in a way that results in something *new*.

True dialogue, in which one person intentionally *listens* to another and expects meaning and truth to emerge, is not possible if the partners rigidly hold to their original positions. In true dialogue, the end result of the "to-and-fro" of conversation (Gadamer) is always something new that changes both partners for a time. They can no longer view the world in exactly the same way. In this mode, truth and meaning are not just abstract principles by which we pattern our lives; they *emerge* out of interaction, and are always dynamic.

Our relationship with youth is complex, powerful, and ever new. The church needs to begin a new relationship with youth, engaging them in true dialogue, fully giving them their due as persons with claims to truth and meaning. They can contribute something mean-

Faith Development 61

ingful to our common life in the church and in the world. We will not be successful in our relationships with youth if we regard them as incomplete, immature "potential adults." We must trust God to allow what *emerges* from the interaction to be fresh, new, and in keeping with God's continuing self-revelation and will for the world.

Engaging youth seriously as dialogue partners may be frightening. Youth view the world differently, and many adults find that scary. The interaction becomes dangerous only when one culture dominates and places a lid on the other. An open, sharing, respectful, dialogue between youth and adults in the church has the potential to help us appropriate God's presence in the world in a new, meaningful, and productive way. Ministry in the coming age must begin to open itself to just such dialogue.

An important understanding is that youth who would make good candidates for ministry *happen*. They arise out of a complex relationship involving their own personalities: the role of meaningful relationships with persons who function as "guarantors;" the interaction of the youth culture and the church culture; a sense of the need of persons for ministry; an awareness of their own talents and gifts; and the role of God's presence in the Spirit. Those who work with youth cannot create ministers! Potential ministers emerge out of an intricate mix of factors.

It is apparent that adolescence is a critical time in a person's life. It is critical not only in relation to one's intellectual, emotional, social, and physical development, but also in relation to one's faith formation. It is a time of great change and massive developmental leaps. It is a time in which individuals potentially become conscious of themselves, others, and the world, including some of the world's hurts and hungers.

Perhaps the perception of the critical nature of adolescence is responsible for the difficulty experienced by the church as it struggles with the presence of youth within its community, which often manifests itself as pervasive fear of youth:

— a fear of what we (adults) do not know about the youth culture and what youth really think;

— a fear which recognizes that much is at stake; that we must "retain" youth within the life of the church;

— a fear which reminds adults that they are aging;

— a fear that prompts a negative, ineffective, or non-productive response.

It is no surprise that adult members of the community often express this fear as anger and resentment. Resentment is revealed as adults insulate themselves from these "uncomfortable" members of the community. Insulation occurs as youth are separated from the ongoing community of faith, and is expressed in the language of exclusion: the youth room, doing youth work, the youth program, youth Sunday. As youth are insulated from the broader life of the church and are "programmed," they are denied their own experiences and expressions of faith. Rarely is the motive "to exclude" youth intentionally, but the effect is the same. The church and its adult leaders are cautioned to avoid models that reflect this resentment and exclusion.

We stand at a time when the ministry of the church is growing older. Where can fresh meaning be found? Who will speak to this time? What can the church do? A strategy for responding to this situation within the life of the church consists of three components: the active presence of the church with youth, the examination of the church's mission and ministry, and the consideration of current models and value of youth ministry.

Most current models of ministry do not lend themselves to being present with youth. Adolescence is seen as a God-forsaken stage of life, and ministry with them has low priority. The average length of employment for youth ministers in any one position is one and one-half years. Youth are powerless within society, so those who minister with youth are seen as powerless. In addition youth ministers are perceived as preparing for "real ministry" and hence as not quite adult. The church does not value all its ministries equally, it mirrors the value hierarchies of its society. The most experienced, seasoned, and mature are elevated to pulpit ministries. Even the successful minister with youth is "bumped up" to a more "important" ministry of the church.

How should the church minister with youth? It needs to be present with them, wherever youth are found. It must recognize their place within the life of the church and allow them to receive respect and care. As with anyone, the key is to be present and to reflect with them on their life, their culture, and their experience—to find God's hand within the fabric of their life and culture.

If we want youth to be involved in the leadership of the church, then youth have to know the church's mission and know its purpose. Who and what is the church today? What are we asking youth to lead? Does the church manifest the universality of classes, races, and cultures? Youth are watching for the church to be what it claims to be. If the church embodies its claims through significant acts of faith, through service as a witness to the gospel of grace forgiveness, and hope, these acts will speak to them. Such a church will be present where youth are in their culture. It will inspire, motivate, and enable youth to participate. No matter what their ages, such a church will lead them to a maturity of faith and challenge them to participate as ministers in the service of God and Christ. The challenge does not belong to youth but to the church.

The Developmental Emphasis

Developmental theory is based on the premise that human change and growth occur in fairly predictable patterns over a lifetime. According to the "epigenetic" principle, each "part" of the personality has its own special time ascendancy. Maturity depends upon the proper development in the proper sequence of each part. Based on this principle, Erik Erikson charted eight stages of development through the life cycle. Each succeeding stage is predicated by a developmental crisis, out of which the person must synthesize both positive and negative elements. When the conflict is resolved in a constructive way, a particular positive quality is built into the person, and it enhances ongoing development. But if the crisis persists, or is resolved unsatisfactorily, a negative quality creeps in and interferes with ongoing development.

In the stage perspective, the human life cycle brings a series of normative transitions that interrelate (1) inner "laws" of development (biological, psychological, etc.); (2) outer social and cultural influences; and (3) idiosyncratic responses of particular individuals. These transitions occur in such predictable patterns that they are called stages. Anticipated developmental transitions are called "scheduled crises;" they are normally expected to occur. For instance, we commonly refer to the "adolescent identity crisis" and the "mid-life crisis."[32]

All human growth and change occur with varying degrees of continuity and discontinuity. Often, important growth occurs to persons out of intense crisis, especially when there are communal resources available to help the individual negotiate the crisis. In one Oriental language, the word for crisis translates as "dangerous opportunity." Crisis is a pivotal concept in virtually all developmental theories. It refers to the developmental changes and challenges that are normatively expected to accompany a person's journey through a lifetime.

Crises occur with varying degrees of intensity, upheaval, and duration. On occasion, the crisis is experienced as an intense event rather than a gradual process. The more intense the inner turmoil and conflict, the more likely the crisis will have an event-quality, and will be visible to the person and his or her community. Crises have a transforming outcome when the "ingredients" for resolution do not lie in antecedents of the past, but rather derive from a novel inbreaking. This in turn, breaks one out of previous self-world understandings into a new way of seeing life. For many persons, the resolution of intense crisis is filled with religious and spiritual significance. It is felt to be a grace-filled event, the work of the Spirit.

Even faith is today considered a developmental phenomenon. James Fowler's work on faith is based on the structural-development school of thought, which employs a stricter notion of stage progression than do other life-cycle theories. The theory claims that the stages occur in a sequential, invariant, and hierarchical fashion. In terms of psychodynamic theory (and other schools of thought), faith "development" is not as neat and orderly as structural theory might lead us to assume. Growth in faith is comprised of a series of fits and starts, reversals, wanderings, and awakenings over the course of a lifetime. It is not a linear matter. The biblical notion of *being faithful* is more important than the ability to give a cognitive account of one's faith in terms of stages (structures). It is more appropriate, hence, to speak of faith's formation (and transformation), rather than its "development."

The role of crisis in the faith formation of adolescence cannot be overestimated. Some theorists suggest that we spend far more time in-between stages than we do in the stages proper. It is safe to claim that it is not the stages themselves but rather the transitions that are paramount during adolescence. Because stage transitions are predicated by crises, it is important to understand the role they play, as well as their psychodynamics.

A developmental crisis may extend over a period of months or years. The individual may be more recognizable in crisis during certain periods than others. Crises have three distinct phases: entry (abrupt or gradual), duration, and resolution. Sometimes the onset is traced to a specific event, but often it is an imperceptible process. Whatever their catalyst, life crises *happen*; people do not choose to undergo them.

A strong sense of self-identity is never a static or unchangeable achievement. It is a "forever-to-be-revised sense of the reality of the Self within social reality." Though the identity crisis is most pronounced during adolescence, its reconfirmation and redefinition is apparent during other important life transitions, such as marriage, parenthood, divorce, career changes, serious illness, tragic loss, widowhood, unemployment, retirement, and the onset of limitations in old age.

Identity formation involves the production of a meaningful self-concept through which the person links together her or his past, present, and future. The person must be helped to ask and answer: "Who am I?" "Where did I come from?" "Where am I going?" "What and who do I wish to become over the course of my lifetime?" The formation of self-identity begs for effective role models; for family and communal traditions; for mentoring and direct feedback; for permission to try, question, adopt, and discard possibilities; for recognition and ritualizing of progress; for peer support; for firm adult guidance; for exposure to clear value systems and religious beliefs; for rich, structured, yet flexible environments.

The reality of "teenagers in crisis" is well-documented.[33] Disciples youth are no exception. For instance, Search Institute found that at the 7th and 8th grades, about a quarter of Disciples youth had thought about suicide, and by 11th and 12th grades, almost half had. Their reported experiences of sexual intercourse by 11th and 12th grades is among the highest of the denominations studied. Disciples youth also report a heavy use of alcohol at grades 7 and 8. Whereas their use of marijuana is low in those grades, they reportedly "make up for it later." Regarding the Institute's "at-risk index" (including depression, suicide, alcohol use, drugs, aggression, theft, trouble in school, sexual intercourse), 38% of Disciple youth report three or more at-risk behaviors.[34]

By not paying attention to the needs of identity formation, we have left youth vulnerable. At the same time our society exposes youth to more powerful stressors than any generation ever faced. Our whole culture is caught in the crossfire of the old philosophy of self-denial and delayed gratification as the road to maturity, and that of self-fulfillment and instant gratification as the path to a meaningful life. Many sociologists notice a regressive, narcissistic side to youth culture today (obtained from culture at large). Many adolescents have been caught into "premature affluence." They have grown accustomed to high, unrealistic levels of discretionary income that are impossible to maintain during the years of college and early career.

Social commentators have observed fundamental changes in the basic life goals of entering college students. Whereas in the early

1970s the most cherished value was "developing a meaningful philosophy of life" (basic to identity formation!), by 1989 that value had dropped to ninth place. The first choice now is "being well-off financially."[35] Fewer and fewer students are using the college years as a resource for working out who they are and what kind of human beings they ought to be or what vocations are worthy of pursuit. Instead, they choose courses and degree programs geared to achieving their goals of money, power, and status. They have been socialized into a culture of consumerism and instant gratification.

The role of the community that guides adolescents, especially the church, is *not* to minimize the adolescent identity crisis, but to help focus it and provide resources for its creative, healthy resolution.

Healthy conflict resolution depends not only upon cultural, social, and religious resources, but also upon on a psychodynamic process that makes use of human imagination and creativity. The way is led by intuitive grouping. Creativity is a process founded in the imagination; it involves processes that are conscious and unconscious, affective and cognitive, active and passive, somatic and intellectual. It involves struggling and searching, sometimes not even knowing for what.

Creative crisis resolution follows a dynamic, patterned process, beginning in the conscious struggle with a felt, existential conflict. The conflict casts the person into inner and outer turmoil, restlessness, and searching. Out of the long, baffling struggle, there eventually emerges new insight. Sometimes it comes piecemeal. But often it comes with such force or jolt that it feels like a divine "zap." It is the "aha!" moment. Working out the "answer" or insight usually happens piecemeal as well. An important step in this dynamic process is the release of all the tension and energy that was invested in the crisis. Again, the release can be sudden and dramatic, or can occur piecemeal. When intense and dramatic, it is fraught with emotion or physical accompaniments (literally, a "warmed heart" experience).

This process is the core dynamic in intense religious experiences, which are not uncommon during adolescence. It is important that the church take seriously the religious experiences of adolescents and not downplay them as emotional froth. Authentic religious experience is not "heat without light," and so the church can help youth interpret and respond to the new insight (theologically speaking, *revelation!*) received through the experience. While emotional accompaniments are a valid and natural part of adolescent religious experience, youth leaders must be careful not to play into the hands of the anti-intellectual bias present in the church today.

Intense religious experiences often occur during a person's twenties or thirties, as the closure or resolution to a conflicted, delayed adolescence. It is not uncommon for the religious experience to compel the person to reactivate church membership after a lengthy moratorium. Commonly, the person interprets the religious experience as a call to ordained ministry. Whether the individual is actually equipped for church leadership is another matter! The church would be in a better position to help persons sort out the meaning of intense religious experiences if it took seriously the priesthood of all believers and provided better paths of preparation for lay vocations. In any case, inner experience (H. R. Niebuhr called it the "secret call") must be tested against the "ecclesial call." In some cases, the experience is better understood as a call into the general rather than ordained ministry of the church. Vast numbers of persons entering seminary today are prompted by a sense of call based on crisis resolution and have bypassed, at least temporarily, the ecclesial call. The church today seems to be groping for a way to reverse this situation, and to strengthen the role of the ecclesial call.

Present Models, New Directions in Youth Ministry

We explored a number of models of youth ministry and became aware of a number of problems with each model. The key issues were their inadequate understanding of adolescence and their lack of comprehending the complexity and pluralism of the world. Most theories of youth ministry focus only on the individual, offering simplistic descriptions of the nature of the person and culture, resulting in equally simplistic solutions. We need a model that takes youth culture seriously, that underscores the relationship of youth to the hurts and hungers of the wider cultural context. Youth need to read and respond to the larger world in which they live in light of the Christian Story and Vision.

Another key issue for youth ministry, and hence for the call to ordained ministry, is getting youth out of the *cul de sacs* of their Protestant middle class culture, and out of the gathered institutional church, and into the public world with its systemic issues. This latter concern is especially overlooked in current approaches to youth ministry.

Dean Hoge's survey results, comparing white and Black Protestant youth, emphasizes the need for an alternative approach.

White church leaders might reflect on the weaker church commitment felt by white youth; the sources behind it are difficult to identify and even more difficult to influence. Also the white youth, who feel less compassion for the poor, might benefit from experiences providing direct contact with the poor and hungry. Whether they feel religious motivation to undertake social witness, or at least to re-evaluate their attitudes, is uncertain, since the requisite religious motivation is not always in place. Many have no interest, given the look-out-for-number-one mentality fashionable in the 1980's. So they should be exposed to social reality and to the Christian teachings about social responsibility, community life, and the common good whenever possible.[36]

Attempting to counteract the reality exposed by Hoge, some youth ministry models attempt, yet fail, to get youth out of their cultural *cul de sacs* and expose them to social reality. This fact is detected, for instance, in Charles Foster's comparison of church versus para-church oriented youth ministries.

Recent writings on youth ministry indicate at least two dominant approaches to the social character of adolescence. For *church-oriented* interpreters like David Ng, Jeffrey D. Jones and Michael Warren, the context of youth ministry is "in the church." As such what they emphasize is evoked by Warren's description of the "ideal context" for the kind of youth ministry he envisions as an intergenerational community, modeling active commitment to justice out of religious faith. Youth participate in the ministry of the church consequently as "full members" and not as "members in training."...

In contrast, the so-called *para-church* interpreters of youth ministry locate the context of their efforts in the school.[37]

Let us make two observations here. In the first place, youth ministry focused on the "in-the-church-context" rarely gets to the world and its culture because the church itself has major problems with this relationship, even though David Ng's and Michael Warren's writings creatively and significantly include justice and cultural issues. And, secondly, while the "in-the-school-context" transcends the parochialism of the church, it addresses only *one* sector of the culture, the school and its peer group life, and that from the narrow perspective of personal salvation.

Rites of Passage Youth Ministry: An Alternative (hereafter called ROPYM)[38] situates the Christian journey within the larger context of life and culture. In the ROPYM model, youth are given experiences in four areas of life, in addition to those usually occurring with youth: (1) *in the adult work world* through choosing one area of adult work a year to experience through field trips, e.g. the field of health care; (2) *with marginal persons* in the local community, e.g. persons in a teenage shelter or in an institution for the mentally handicapped; (3) *with other classes and cultures*, e.g. through a field trip to a large city; and (4) *in the world of nature*, e.g. through camping trips. These, in addition to their home, school, work, and peer experiences, are "critically reflected" upon and related to the Story and Vision of the Christian faith.

We would argue that "rites of passage youth ministry" provides a vehicle by which youth ministry can affirm the genuine insights of both the church-oriented and para-church approaches. It can also relate to the systemic issues and institutions of culture, as well as to the issues of identity formation. The discussion of the ROPYM model is not intended to be, at least for the purposes of this report, the prescriptive model for youth ministry in the Christian Church (Disciples of Christ). In the context of this report, ROPYM is used to illustrate one way the church can help nurture in persons the capacities and competencies needed for quality ordained leadership of the church in the world today. Churches could, for instance, adopt the emphases of the ROPYM model without taking it on in its entirety.

The pilgrimage of youth is comprehended, both *communally* and *personally*, as a journey *down into* the matrix of Creation and history, understood in terms of the communities and experiences of our whole culture with its organizations and institutions, as well as with nature. The gathered community of the church is the keeper and teacher of the Christian Story and Vision, where the Story is caught as well as taught by participation in a community of faith with adult members. The Story needs to be taught in such a way that youth are enabled to "exegete" the structures, dynamics, and dimensions of the persons and networks through which they are journeying and through which God is actively working: the adult work world, marginal persons, other classes and cultures, and nature.

What are the similarities and differences between the Rites of Passage approach and conventional approaches to youth ministry? They all are concerned (1) about the formation of Christians within community; and (2) about youth acquiring the Christian Story.

However, ROPYM involves young people in the communities and institutions of the adult work world, and in cultural and social worlds that are different from their own. These experiences address key aspects of identity formation: What am I going to be when I grow up? What tasks are there in the world that call forth my gifts and graces in light of the Realm of God? How am I called, as a responsible person (teenager and then adult) to respond to the systemic, as well as the personal, sin in the world in light of the Christian Story?

Experiences *outside* the ordinary world of the teenager increase the knowledge and consciousness of adolescents as no reading or media experience can. Experience in the adult work world and in social worlds other than their own also address the plea of many adults about getting youth involved with and concerned about political and social issues. Just as importantly, it gives them realistic experiences to ground their thinking about *what* education and training will be necessary to respond to their call as Christians: Should I go to college or vo-tech? What should my major be? These experiences raise questions about (a) their vocation, (b) the relationship of the Christian faith to the world, as well as (c) the call to ordained Christian ministry.

While most youth programs focus only on commitment to Jesus Christ and/or becoming responsible members of the church, ROPYM equips youth with experience and language to relate the biblical Story to the broader, yet concrete, environment of creations and history. Since most churches have difficulty witnessing to Jesus Christ (reconciliation, love, and justice) within the world, the youth program (as well as the adult ministry) often becomes Jesus-and ecclesio-centric. ROPYM directly engages youth with the public as well as the interpersonal world.

Issues of Youth Ministry in a Friendship Metaphor

The center of gravity of all youth ministry, including ROPYM, is where *Friendship* is pivotal, and relationships are dialogical and interpersonal. *Becoming a person, with others, in a community which knows the Christian Story, and where one is affectively related to the God of that story, is the key conversion point of formation and transformation* within the Christian faith.

Because Middle Protestantism is critical of moralism and pietism, and theologically educates its ministers in an abstract interpretation of the Story, few Middle Protestant ministers affirm the central importance of a personal and affective relationship with God in Jesus

Christ (piety or spirituality).[39] Consequently, the experience of conversion and genuine piety is looked upon askance and not affirmed.

The transition between the second and third stages in faith development can be understood as the fundamental conversion from legalism to grace, expressed in interpersonal terms between God and a youth (between Jesus Christ and a youth). Even though this is the specialty of the para-church groups and "fundamentalists," it needs to be recaptured in appropriate ways by Middle Protestantism. The real problem with conversion is not piety itself, but rather with piety reduced to Jesus-ology, individualism, and moving beyond Stage Three. *Middle Protestantism needs to reaffirm personal relationship with God* (piety or spirituality) as central *to this stage of the pilgrimage of faith.*

The third stage is characterized by the formation of community, especially the interpersonal life of small groups. Opportunities for dialogue and exchanging one's story can take almost any form. In Christian community human interpersonal exchange is linked with God-person interaction. The "empowerment" of youth is significantly related to this stage of formation in community.

Unfortunately, many youth ministries become self-oriented, and fail to understand that the Christian faith entails a mission. Yet even when mission is affirmed, it is often conceived in limited terms, such as youth choir, participation in the committees of the church, or increasing youth fellowship membership. Youth programs with a mission program "outside" the church are also conceived in traditional terms: work with the less fortunate (charity in the bad sense), trips to church missions, and so on. ROPYM structures mission in terms of engagement with and awareness of public and cultural life. Yet also within these contexts personal issues of identity-formation, friendship, relationship with parents, and the meaning of life are addressed.

Recommendations

The suggestions listed below point to the kind of educational environment and youth ministry that we believe important to sustain a Christian community out of which young people may hear and respond to the call to ordained ministry. Other recommendations are implicit throughout the report.

In seeking to enhance the quality of its ordained leadership, and to strengthen its overall faithfulness to God's mission—

1. ....*the church should emphasize the vocational calling of all Christians, bestowed in their baptism.* This emphasis would provide the fundamen-

tal context out of which to draw and set aside ("call") ordained leadership. When the church takes seriously the ministry of all Christians, that is, the congregational in contrast to the clergy paradigm of ministry, then it provides the necessary environment out of which particular individuals are set aside for ordained leadership. In the congregational paradigm, the leadership of ordained ministry is understood to be focused on creating a context wherein all Christians may discover and use their gifts and graces for significant ministry in the world.

2. *...the church should recognize the traditional distinctions of "call" to ministry.* In his classic work, *The Purpose of the Church and its Ministry: Reflections on the Aims of Theological Education,*[40] H. R. Niebuhr describes four dimensions of the call to ministry. Throughout the history of the church, varying degrees of importance have been attached to each of these modes of calling. They are: (1) the call to be a Christian; (2) the secret call, an inner persuasion or experience wherein the individual feels personally called by God into the work of Christian ministry; (3) the providential call, a discernment of particular intellectual, psychological, moral, and physical gifts to carry on tasks associated with ordained leadership; and (4) the ecclesiastical call, the public invitation extended by the church to be one of its ordained leaders.

For Gregory the Great and for Chrysostom, for example, the providential call was of foremost importance, followed by the ecclesiastical call. That is, the church discerned in certain individuals the gifts and graces for ministry (the providential call), and then summoned those persons into the church's ordained ministry (the ecclesiastical call). This assumed a lively sense of the ministry of all baptized Christians (the Christian call). The inner confirmation (the secret call) usually came after the church call.

It may be that the church abdicated its role in the calling of persons to ordained ministry, and is now coming to grips with that fact. The challenge the church faces, however, is not to manipulate or mechanize the process.

3. *...the church should attend to the formation of Christian community, especially through small, face-to-face groups.* The formation of Christian community, especially the life of small groups, where there is dialogue, care, and sharing of one's story, is crucial for experiencing love, acceptance, hope, forgiveness, and the Holy Spirit, all necessary to the Christian life, and responding to God's call to Christian ministry, especially ordained leadership.

Search Institute reports that Disciples youth give comparatively high marks to their churches, in contrast to other mainline youth, for helping them to love life and feel concern for others.[41] The Institute findings also indicate that an important factor in effective Christian education for youth is having a high percentage of their peers involved in education. Other factors in local churches that help youth mature in faith include: (a) a warm climate in the congregation, where members are perceived to be friendly; (b) a sense of being family, including the degree to which youth personally experience the care and concern of the congregation; (c) an intergenerational emphasis in programming; and (d) the quality of Sunday worship, where all ages are involved.

4. *...the church should affirm and cultivate a lively sense of spirituality (piety) in adolescents.* This will include recovering within middle Protestantism the experience of *conversion* from legalism to grace (from sin to Jesus Christ), which is a special emphasis of the parachurch groups, the conservatives, and the fundamentalists. Developmentally, this is the transition from the second to the third stages. The personal relationship with God in Jesus Christ is central to the pilgrimage of faith, and is especially needed by adolescents who yearn for a "cosmic face (friend) that never goes away." As pointed out above, developmental transitions are often predicated by intense religious experience, and so the church needs to appreciate such experience, and assist young people in reflecting on and integrating their experiences into their ongoing faith journey.

Search Institute reports that Disciples youth, along with Disciples adults, give high rank to learning about the spiritual life, as well as improving their relational skills.[42] Unfortunately, the survey reveals that more than two-thirds of Disciples youth have an "undeveloped" faith. Also, their faith is expressed more horizontally (relationships with others) than vertically (relationship with God or Jesus Christ). This highlights the need for more attention to the spiritual life.

5. *...the church should recognize and ritualize the place of Christian mentors.* While dialogue between members of the youth group is primary, our conclusion, after sharing personal journeys, is that one of the most important factors leading youth to respond to the call to ministry is a relationship with a specific mentor who has been formed, informed, and transformed by the Christian Story. The adult discerned the youth's capacities and abilities, and suggested the possibility of Christian ministry as a vocation. Both Christian community and a particular quality of mentoring are essential. In giving more attention to Christian initiation (e.g., investing more time and

energy in the traditional "pastor's class"), the church can provide each young person with a mentor in the congregation (perhaps an Elder called a "faith friend") who will spend quality time with the young person. As David Elkind points out:

> In the autobiographies of many men and women who became successful despite adversity, one repeatedly finds that a significant person in their lives recognized their special gifts and devoted time, energy, and skill to helping them realize their abilities.[43]

The role of mentors in the congregation is closely tied to the pastor's role in "sponsoring" the faith formation of youth. The pastor ideally will (a) be highly committed to educational programming for youth; (b) devote significant time to the youth program; and (c) know educational theories and practices related to effective Christian education for youth.[44] Search Institute confirms what has long been suspected: that teachers and pastors are very important influences in the faith maturity of adolescents.

Parents of young people should also be encouraged to think of themselves as their child's mentor in the faith. According to Search Institute, the two most important factors associated with faith maturity in youth are (a) the degree of family religiousness, and (b) the sheer amount of exposure to Christian education. The most powerful positive correlate of a young person's faith maturity is conversation about God and faith with one's mother during the childhood ages of 5 through 12. Another powerful correlate is talking with one's father about faith and God, and talking to other friends and relatives. Closely related is the experience of family devotions and family involvement in helping others.[45] This suggests the need for the church to help families find ways in their home life to nurture faith, and to engage together in Christian service to the world.

6. *....the church should give young people "tools" by which to discern and participate in God's work in the world.* A Christian community oriented to a significant, non-paternalistic kind of *mission* is important for ministry with youth. Because research indicates that so many church members are locked into a narrow, conventional, individualistic understanding of faith, youth ministry can emphasize getting young people out of the church building and into significant places in the world where God's redemptive work is discerned.

The approach to youth ministry recommended in this chapter, thus, sharply differs with the increasingly popular "church participation model" where youth are engaged in the life of the local church (on committees, assisting in worship, etc.) and where the Christian faith is experienced mostly in its gathered form. One problem with the church participation model is that so little of the life of the gathered church is "in the world," or in mission to, with, and for the victims, problems, and systems of this world. Another is that few theological "tools" are taught with which to "exegete" the world and its cultures.

According to Search Institute, Disciples youth do not feel their churches involve them in helping the poor and others in need, or in spending time with other races and ethnic groups.[46] On the whole, members of our denomination have placed "social issues" at the bottom of their priority lists. This makes it incumbent upon us to help youth and adults apply their faith to political and social issues, and to the meaning of systemic oppression and injustice.[47] Programming in Christian education for youth, therefore, will include: (a) involving youth in service projects; (b) teaching youth responsibility for addressing poverty and hunger; (c) helping youth develop concern for other persons; (d) teaching moral decision-making skills.[48]

7. *...the church should help young people grasp the basic narrative of the Christian Story.* The Christian Story must be understood in its narrative, almost literal, form before its deeper aspects can be interpreted. Consequently, churches that are concerned about biblical and theological literacy among their youth must teach the Story *before* it can be understood and related to life, i.e., in grade school and junior high school (as well as in high school and later on). Search Institute confirms that, ideally, Christian education for youth will include teaching the Bible and teaching core theological concepts.

Knowing the Christian Story is imperative so that youth have an understanding of God, Christ, persons, and church enabling them to enter dialogue with the world. Even a literal understanding of the Story and doctrine is important ("religion" in John Westerhoff's terms). Stories, timeliness, facts, etc. about the Christian tradition are important carriers of its meaning. At each stage of the journey other dimensions of understanding the Story can be added, but without knowing basic biblical stories there is nothing to interpret. This affirmation of the role of "literalism" relates both to the importance of "getting the story" *before* adolescence, and to the *continuance* of "religion" as a framework for understanding the Christian faith. Therefore, some aspects of youth ministry can be (should be) the unapologetic acquisition of this kind of content.

8. *...the church should spend time with youth where they are, in places, moments, and ways where youth culture is mediated.* If youth are to be

included within the faith community, it is called to be present *with* them. If youth culture is the primary scene of their recognition of grace, forgiveness, and hope, the church is called to be present there. The church thus needs to spend more time *with* youth: going to school, attending athletic events, watching MTV, reading their literature, listening, sharing, asking about their ideas, seeking their advice as members of Christ's church today. If youth are to respond to a call to ordained ministry, then the church is called to be familiar enough with youth to issue such a call. Youth respond when they are known and loved. Youth will respond when they are recognized as gifted and graced for bearing witness to God's presence in all the world.

The church, therefore, must recognize the "real world" in which youth live, and help them deal with it. The *way* Christian education is done makes a vital difference to whether young people mature in their faith. For instance, in addition to the other emphases, ministry with youth will include education about human sexuality, and drugs and alcohol, and help youth make decisions about them.

9. *...the church should help leaders acquire a repertoire of methods by which to help youth critically reflect on their culture and the larger culture.* To consider adolescent faith formation is to consider young people in their own culture. We cannot abstract them from it. What, though, is the criteria by which to discern the good stuff going on in youth culture? How can we immerse ourselves in youth culture sufficiently to help young people critically reflect upon it? The church is called to struggle with these questions.

The church must help young people see what questions their culture poses to their faith and self-identity. To teach youth to read, resist, revise their culture is to initiate them into the counter-cultural way of life that Christianity is.

The church is also called to struggle with ways to help youth critically reflect on the larger, dominant culture as part of their initiation into Christian vocation in the world. "Rites of passage youth ministry" is one way to approach this task. The important thing is for the church to make this a priority if it intends to sponsor persons toward greater faith maturity.

10. *...the church should revitalize and renew its whole educational ministry as the proper context out of which to call young persons into full-time ministry.* Alongside the need for the church to invest itself in the calling of youth into ordained ministry is the need to be concerned about the shape of youth ministry in particular, and educational ministry in general. Search Institute emphasizes that the two stron-

gest correlates of faith maturity are: the amount of exposure to Christian education throughout a lifetime, and family religiousness (including the family's involvement in helping others). Educational involvement, particularly during late adolescence, promotes positive movement toward greater faith maturity.[49] While effective education for youth requires particular kinds of process, content, leadership, and administration, many of these factors are lacking in the local churches. Formal Christian education includes:

> Sunday School, church school, Bible studies, confirmation, camping, retreats, workshops, youth ministry and youth groups, children and adult choirs, auxiliaries for men and women, prayer groups, religious plays and dramas, Vacation Bible School, new member classes, and intergenerational or family events and programs....[Informal education includes] the values, symbols, culture, and patterns of interaction that help describe congregational life.[50]

> There is another related finding. Those denominations that are *more formal* (in liturgy and/or doctrine), and that have *less lay participation* in worship, also have a lower percentage of members with "integrated faith." The less formal denominations, including Disciples of Christ, show a higher percentage of members with an integrated faith.

These findings seem to suggest several hypotheses *vis-a-vis* this project. Firstly, believer's baptism should continue to be an important "rite of passage" for Disciples and, perhaps, greater attention should be given to preparing persons for it. Also, there needs to be more investment in the manner in which it is done. Secondly, liturgical informality with high degrees of lay participation may be a very important way of engendering a mature, integrated faith.

Overall, one of the most important things the church can do is simply spend time with youth. Lack of relationship between youth and the church appeared in many forms in the Institute's findings (including Disciples). Youth sensed they were not cared for. There was low adult participation in Christian education, little time given to "at risk" youth, lack of intergenerational events, and a low degree of "faith conversation" in families. Youth themselves showed low interest in "getting to know adults in my church."

The comprehensive youth ministry approach commended in this report does not address the call to ordained ministry directly, but it demonstrates a broader understanding of the purpose and mission of the church, and calls youth to the task of Christ transforming persons as well as culture. Within this broader and deeper engagement with systems and structures, *some youth* will be called into professional ministry.

5

Changing North American Demographics

The 1990s present various challenges to the Christian Church (Disciples of Christ), the responses to which will undoubtedly influence the ministries of the church for generations to come. Foremost among these challenges is the increasingly multicultural profile of the United States population. Projected demographics indicate that the fastest growing segments of the population are non-whites, including non-native born minorities (e.g. Central American immigrants). Currently the Christian Church (Disciples of Christ) has not extended its ministry significantly among these groups. For example, while the state of California has almost nine million Hispanics, as of this writing there were are only two established Hispanic Disciples congregations in the Pacific Southwest Region.

If we are to extend our outreach among these growing ethnic and cultural minorities we must become more realistic and effective in our recruitment and education of persons who will have the capacity to minister to congregations among these groups.

Our assignment was to report on the status and prospects for ministry among the racial/ethnic minorities within the Christian Church (Disciples of Christ) and to make recommendations for the future. We employed a variety of methods in an effort to fulfill our assignment. Members of the team engaged in consultations with Ozark Range, Sr., Harold Johnson, and Luis Ferrer, who carried responsibilities within the general manifestation of the church for oversight respectively of African-American, American-Asian and Hispanic clergy and congregations among Disciples. We have also conferred with James Powell, director of new church establishment for the denomination, and Mrs. D. Lee Putnam of the Pension Fund. Three members of our Team prepared papers on two of the three groups presented in this chapter![51] We talked at length by telephone and met twice to share and check out our findings. The chair held individual conferences with team members to facilitate the gathering

80   *Discerning the Call*

of information and the writing of the report. We consulted studies on theological preparation of African-American and Hispanic Disciples in the United States (see endnotes 57 and 54 for names of the documents).

We note at the outset that a report on racial/ethnic minorities among the Disciples must recognize the distinctive situation characterizing each of the diverse groups. Their histories and present situations are quite different. Furthermore, their self-consciousness and concern to preserve their unique identities are increasing in American society and within the church.

African-Americans are perhaps the most homogeneous among the minority groups, and even there, among Disciples, are notable differences between rural and urban and between churches supporting full-time leadership and the majority whose pastors hold other full-time positions. Hispanic Americans reflect different national origins with distinctive traditions. Puerto Ricans are concentrated primarily in the northeast; Mexicans in the cities of the southwest and Pacific Southwest; Central and South Americans are scattered in many places but have a concentration in Florida where one Disciples congregation has more than twenty nationalities represented in its membership. Asians are differentiated by countries of origin, languages, and periods of immigration. As a result of this wide diversity, we will make a few generalizations about the future needs of ministry among them as a whole and also try to make clear the particular prospects for each group.

We wish to register two concerns that arose during our research. The first is the absence of complete and coordinated data sources for the ministry among the Disciples. No one office appears to have responsibility for keeping an up-to-date and comprehensive file on those who are recognized as ministers. Furthermore, some information is not available. As an example, we have birthdates only for those who are members of the Pension Fund. Thus the majority of African-American ministers are not included in assessing rates of retirement. Also, because of our historic reluctance to identify each other by ethnic origin, our study may have overlooked some who should have been included. We had to look for Hispanic and Asian surnames among lists of ministers and rely on those who work with those groups.

The second concern is our frustration at the absence of structures through which the concerns of the racial/ethnic groups are regularly addressed.[52] This is especially true for Hispanics and Asians. The

Disciples "establishment" still relates to these groups on an *ad hoc* basis for the most part. It continues to feel that they are outsiders and have not been made a part of the organized life of the church through regional and general manifestations.

In the report which follows we will first look at some demographic data regarding each group, to learn about areas of growth, education and economic levels, and other social characteristics. We will then describe something of the Disciples present situation among the groups. Finally we will set out some recommendations regarding the future need for ministers among the groups, including education and financial support.

Who We Are and Where We Are

1) African-Americans are now largely an urban people; more than four in five live in metropolitan areas. See the table below for areas with populations more than 500,000.

(Numbers are in thousands)

Rank	Metropolitan Area	Population 1980	1985	Percent Increase	Proportion Black 1980	1985
1	New York CMSA	2,941	3,201	8.8	16.9	18.1
2	Chicago CMSA	1,564	1,645	5.2	19.7	20.3
3	Los Angeles CMSA	1,065	1,194	12.1	9.3	9.2
4	Philadelphia CMSA	1,044	1,109	6.2	18.4	19.2
5	Washington D.C. MSA	874	965	10.3	26.9	27.3
6	Detroit CMSA	921	949	3.1	19.4	20.4
7	Houston CMSA	564	641	13.6	18.2	18.0
8	Atlanta MSA	526	608	15.6	24.6	24.9
9	Baltimore MSA	561	592	5.6	25.5	26.0
10	San Francisco CMSA	471	524	11.2	8.8	8.9

Source: U.S. Bureau of the Census

Cities in which Disciples are relatively strong and in which there are large populations of African-Americans include Atlanta, Houston, Indianapolis, Kansas City, Los Angeles, Memphis (41% African-American), and St. Louis. Between 1980-85, cities experiencing more than 20% growth among African-Americans included Miami, Sacramento, Honolulu, Phoenix, and, in the Los Angeles area, Riverside, Anaheim, and Oxnard.

The urban movement of African-Americans peaked years ago; they are no longer immigrants and strangers to American cities but dwell in well-established enclaves. In the African-American community their sense of solidarity with one another remains strong, and likewise the importance of the Black church in affirming their self-understanding as African-Americans as well as children of God and members of the human family.

2) Hispanic-Americans are the fastest growing ethnic minority in the country. The 1980 Census placed the Hispanic population at 14.6 million persons. In the past nine years, it has grown 62% to 23.7 million persons.[53] All but four million of these live in nine states led by California, Texas, and New York. Over one-half live in metropolitan areas. Most (two-thirds) of the others live in five southwestern states.

It is important to remember that in the southwestern states the Spanish heritage is older than is the Anglo heritage in other areas of the nation. Long before Plymouth Rock and Jamestown, the Spanish missions were spread across the west and southwest. When Mexico gained independence from Spain in 1821, its boundaries included what is now California, Texas, New Mexico, Nevada, Utah, and part of Colorado. When in 1848 the Treaty of Guadalupe Hidalgo awarded the United States all Mexican territory north of the Rio Grande, by the stroke of the pen, the United States gained a vast Spanish heritage, a population instilled in the culture and traditions of Spain. These relatively small Spanish settlements have continued to grow to this day with a steady flow of immigration. It is estimated that during the first three decades of the twentieth century, fully one-tenth of the population of Mexico migrated to the United States.[54]

Metropolitan Areas: 1985 Hispanic Populations Exceeding 200,000

(Numbers are in thousands)

Rank	Metropolitan Area	Population 1980	1985	Percent Increase	Proportion Hispanic 1980	1985
1	Los Angeles CMSA	2,766	3,550	28.3	24.1	28.3
2	New York CMSA	2,045	2,346	14.7	11.7	13.2
3	Miami CMSA	627	815	30.0	23.7	28.3
4	San Francisco CMSA	649	775	19.4	12.1	13.2
5	Chicago CMSA	620	775	25.0	7.8	9.4
6	Houston CMSA	446	595	33.3	14.4	16.7

7	San Antonio MSA	485	568	16.9	45.3	46.5
8	El Paso MSA	300	360	20.0	62.5	67.5
9	San Diego MSA	274	358	30.7	14.7	16.6
10	Dallas CMSA	246	346	40.5	8.4	9.9
11	McAllen TX MSA	232	281	21.0	81.9	82.9
12	Phoenix MSA	200	250	24.9	13.3	13.8
13	Denver CMSA	173	203	17.1	10.7	11.1

Source: U.S. Bureau of the Census

Those of Mexican origin are by far the largest Hispanic group, numbering fourteen and one half million. They also have the highest percentage of US-born (74% in 1980). Puerto Rico and Central/South America are the areas of origin of nearly three million persons. Cuba accounts for over a million three hundred thousand. About one-half the Puerto Ricans living in the continental US have lived here all their lives, whereas only about twenty percent of Cuban and Central/South American residents were born in the US.

COUNTRY OF ORIGIN OF
U.S. HISPANIC POPULATION GROWTH
1980-1989

TOTAL HISPANIC POPULATION

Country/Place of origin	1980 (000)	1989 (000)	# Change (000)	% Change
Mexico	8,740.0	14,609.1	5,869.1	67.2%
Central/South America	1,693.3	2,983.4	1,290.1	76.2
Puerto Rico	2,014.0	2,817.7	803.7	39.9
Cuba	803.0	1,326.0	523.0	65.1
Other Hispanic	1,353.4	1,941.6	588.2	43.5
TOTAL	14,603.7	23,677.8	9,074.1	62.1%

Source: Strategy Research Corp., 1989

Puerto Ricans have settled primarily in the Northeastern United States although more recently there has been a shift to Florida. Even though migration patterns of Mexican-Americans have carried them to most urban areas of the country they remain primarily in the Southwest and Pacific Southwest. Cuban-Americans have settled primarily in Florida, in and around Miami. There are wide economic differences within the Cuban population in this country, reflecting the status of many who were recognized as political refugees receiving government assistance; whereas most of those from Puerto Rico and Mexico have come without government assistance and were seeking economic opportunity. Many recent Central and Latin Americans have come as political refugees seeking asylum often with help from churches providing sanctuary from the US government as well as their own.

For the Hispanic-American population as a whole it is important to note that Spanish language proficiency is almost three times greater than English proficiency. Over 97% of the US Hispanics learned Spanish as their "first language spoken." Spanish language is increasing while English language proficiency has decreased. Hispanics feel strongly about their Hispanic background, and 91% believe that it is very important for their children to read and write Spanish with perfection. Only approximately 13% or 3.1 million are considered fully assimilated. Most of the increase in the Hispanic population in the past decade is accounted for by immigration (approximately 5.6 million). These recent immigrants have contributed to a resurgence of interest in the Hispanic heritage and language. The average age among Hispanic-Americans is 25.7 years, below that for non-Hispanic persons in the US.[55]

The religious situation among Hispanic-Americans is unique and must be taken into account if effective ministry is to be developed among them. Justo Gonzalez has pointed out that although they are Catholic, "much of Catholic spirituality among Hispanics takes the form of cultural Catholicism" and as many as 90% "do not participate in the institutional life of the Church." They are Catholic "in their own fashion."

> There is a deep popular piety that informs all of life. Belief in life after death, in an ultimately moral order, in the saving work of Jesus Christ, and in the final judgment is common among such cultural Catholics.... Popular religiosity, home religion, and a generally Catholic spirituality, while not always institutionalized, often serve as a force of unity among Hispanics.... Hispanic Protestants tend to be very loyal to their congregations, but not necessarily to their denominations.[56]

3) Asian-Americans represent numerous nationalities and languages. Newcomers (first-generation) outnumber older immigrants (second generation) more than two to one (3,770,000 to 1,520,000). (See the following table.) They, too, tend to colonize and find both

language and religion a support to them as they cope with the challenge of making a place for themselves in a new society. The church in North America has often been a place where new peoples affirm their own values and cultures, free from the pressures encountered in their secular lives. This is no different today among Asian-American Disciples.

As the table below makes evident, Koreans and Filipinos are by far the majority of the most recent newcomers. Their coming is motivated by desires both for economic opportunities and freedom from political oppression.

Asian Ethnic Group	Population: 1st Generation	Population: 2nd Generation
Chinese	600,000	450,000
Filipino	1.2 million	400,000
Indonesian	60,000	10,000
Japanese	400,000	350,000
Korean	1.1 million	200,000
Malaysian	60,000	10,000
Vietnamese	200,000	60,000
Thai	150,000	40,000

Source: Rev. Soongook Choi

The Present Situation and Future Prospects of These Groups Among Disciples

1) Dr. Ozark Range reports that there are 535 African-American congregations among the Christian Church (Disciples of Christ) with 450 ministers and approximately 92,000 members. Seventy-seven of the pastors are full time, over one-half have a college degree, and one-fourth hold the Master of Divinity. Many completed college after ordination and nearly all have continued to pursue educational opportunities. Over half the full-time ordained ministers reported in 1985 have an annual salary of less than $15,000 (including benefits) from the congregation, earn a similar amount from another job, and have a spouse who is also employed.[57]

A salary support program administered by the Department of Ministry assists African-American congregations to become "full-time." Since 1973 forty-seven congregations have received such aid. Thirty-five of these are now on their own, paying the salary of a full-time pastor. In 1990, four congregations received salary support ranging from $4,000 to $10,000. To qualify, among other things, the minister "shall have held standing or shall have been under the care of a Commission on the Ministry in the Christian Church (Disciples of Christ) for a minimum of 2 years."

In 1985 twenty-five percent of these pastors were within ten years of retirement age (65) and another twenty-five percent were older than that.[58] One hundred and sixty-five African-American pastors hold membership in the Pension Fund of the Christian Church. Thirty-nine (23.6%) are over 60. An additional 89 receive benefits from the Pension Fund.

African-American Disciples participate fully in the general bodies of the church. In 1985 they constituted thirteen percent of the membership of general church boards and committees and are well represented among staffs.[59] Dr. Allen found that they continue their "struggle with the dichotomy of preserving Black religious heritage and identity while at the same time promoting the true spirit of 'the church,' which is unity."[60]

They are organized in a National Convocation which meets biennially, and hold state missionary conventions in Alabama, Kentucky, South Carolina, Mississippi, Texas, and a Piedmont Tri-State Convention covering Virginia, West Virginia, and parts of North Carolina. In addition, along the eastern seaboard from South Carolina to New Jersey they have district assemblies headed by bishops.

The Division of Homeland Ministries convenes a Black Ministers' Retreat annually and has a Director of Black Ministry located in that unit's Department of Ministry. The director administers the Star Supporter Fund which provides scholarship aid to African-American Disciples who are preparing for ministry. The Convocation continually urges its pastors to participate in continuing education programs and works with other agencies in the denomination to provide educational opportunities for them.

Allen found that 52% of African-American pastors "had not completed college at the time they were first appointed as ministers. Of this number ten percent were less than high school graduates and 28% attended college but did not graduate." Nearly half of those not graduating had participated in special studies of at least one year in duration. Many continue in degree programs, and by the time of the study only 14% had not graduated from college while 38% held graduate degrees. "Eleven percent were seminary graduates, and five percent had graduate (non-seminary) degrees at the time of their first appointment."[61] It is clear that a large majority of these pastors enter ministry prior to educational preparation for ministry. However, it is also clear that they consider education for ministry important to the fulfillment of their calls and are willing to work and sacrifice for additional education.

Allen concluded that there is a "dearth in the enlistment of new ministers among Black Disciples" and a need for organized denominational effort to identify and challenge them. His findings also led to the conclusion that "a large proportion of Black pastors have inadequate theological education, and they have a need for in-service training."[62] They tend also to underutilize the resources of their regional churches.

Thirty-seven African-American Disciples were enrolled in the Master of Divinity degree program during the 1989-90 academic year.

Brite Divinity School	3
Chicago Theological Seminary	1
Christian Theological Seminary	7
School of Theology at Claremont	1
Disciples Divinity House–Chicago	2
Duke Divinity School	4
Eden Theological Seminary	1
Harvard Divinity School	1
Lexington Theological Seminary	5
Memphis Theological Seminary	4
New Brunswick Theological Seminary	2
New York Theological Seminary	1
Perkins School of Theology	1
Phillips Graduate Seminary	2
Pittsburgh Theological Seminary	1
Southeastern Baptist Theo. Seminary	1

(Source: Division of Higher Education)

Over the past six years financial assistance through the Star Supporter Fund has gone to 15 to 16 students annually, the majority of whom are in seminary. The individual grants in 1988 were $1,050 for undergraduates and $1,500 for seminary students. They are funded by gifts from the Christian Men's Fellowships of the denomination and from the Minister's Wives Fellowship of the National Convocation. Forty-five students received grants between 1976 and

88 Discerning the Call

1987. Twenty-one are now in a pastoral ministry, seven in regional or general church ministry, seven in institutional ministry, and six in secular employment leaving only one unaccounted.[63]

One region, Indiana, carries a line item in its budget providing $2,000 to supplement the field education salary of racial/ethnic minority seminarians. This is offered as a grant to congregations employing the student and is crucial because placement opportunities in churches with adequate financial support are few for minority students.

Students finance themselves through a variety of sources including grants from the schools and from the denomination, salaries from field education positions, incomes from secular employment, work-study jobs, loans, and often a combination of all of the above. The school's financial aids officer is usually the central figure when putting together a financial support system for the seminary student.

2) Disciples mission to Hispanics began in 1899 when Primera Iglesia Cristiana was founded in San Antonio, Texas. In the 91 years since the founding of that first Hispanic congregation they have grown to only 46 congregations across the country.

Disciples work with Hispanics through the general manifestation was initiated under Rev. Byran Spice, then of the United Christian Missionary Society. The first Hispanic named to that position was Rev. Domingo Rodriquez of Puerto Rico in 1965. In 1976 an Hispanic Caucus was formed and began to meet with what was then the Committee on Black Concerns. Both groups were united into what became the Committee on Black and Hispanic Concerns which, in 1983, became the Committee on Racial Ethnic Inclusiveness and Empowerment, located under the auspecies of the Office of the General Minister and President, which now also includes Asian-Americans, and serves as an advisory body to all general units of the church.

In 1980 the Hispanics celebrated their first national assembly in Indianapolis. From this first assembly and its consequent work, Hispanic Disciples today are organized into three Hispanic Conventions: one in the Northeast representing 14 churches; one in the Southwest with 16 churches, including 2 from California; one in the Midwest, representing 5 congregations. No Hispanic Convention exists in the Southeast although six new congregations have recently been organized there representing many Central and South American nationalities. A national director of Hispanic Ministries is located in the Department of Evangelism of the Division of Homeland

Ministries. He provides staff services to the Hispanic Convention and to the National Hispanic and Bilingual Fellowship. The Northeastern Region of the Christian Church (Disciples of Christ) employs one staff person part-time to work among Hispanic congregations. There are today approximately fifty active Hispanic clergy in the denomination. Most of those who minister as pastors with congregations are bivocational. An estimated ten to fifteen will be at or near retirement age by the year 2000.

Currently (1989-90) ten Hispanic Disciples are enrolled in seminaries: Brite Divinity School, 1; Christian Theological Seminary, 4; and New York Theological Seminary, 4; and School of Theology at Claremont, 1. Another thirteen are enrolled in various colleges.

Those Disciples ministers who come to the States from Puerto Rico are graduates of Seminario Evangelico De Puerto Rico. They are often in need of in-service training that will help them adapt to inner-city ministries in the US and to face the challenge of ministering to congregations, many of whose members have no Disciples orientation. When Hispanics in the US are called to ministry and come under care of a regional commission on ministry, they are expected to complete a full seminary course.

An Hispanic Scholarship Fund is administered by the Department of Ministry and has assisted four to seven students studying for the ministry each year since 1982. Currently six students receive $1,000 scholarships. All are in seminaries: one junior, four middlers, and one senior.[64]

The goal for the next decade is twenty new, directly-initiated Hispanic congregations. These will be gathered by a pastor/developer employed by the regional and general manifestations. In addition it is expected there will be congregations beginning on their own, people gathering in a home or "nesting" in some Disciples church who will turn to the Director of Hispanic Ministries for counsel. Pastors among these churches will not likely have the educational background or financial possibility to begin a full college and seminary education. They need courses in Spanish offered in the evenings or as short-courses during vacation periods. The Disciples Hispanic Ministry in the Southwest offered such a week of training in Austin, Texas in May of 1990 under the leadership of Dr. Samuel Pagan.

Although Disciples ministry among Hispanics has a long history and has resulted in well established congregations they number, as noted in the previous paragraph, only 46. The new situation as indicated by the demographic data reported earlier in this chapter requires a re-examination of issues of ministerial education and standing for those who minister in Hispanic congregations so as to provide for the growth ahead in ministry among Hispanic people.

3) Today there are ten congregations of Asian-Americans among Disciples. Eight are Korean, one Japanese, and one Filipino. Another sixteen Asian-American Disciples pastors are serving in Anglo congregations: six Filipino, ten Japanese. A Malaysian Disciples minister is chaplain with the Indiana Girls School, a state correctional facility.

In 1983 the denomination recognized a Convocation of Asian-American Disciples. The oversight of Asian-American Disciples work rests at the general manifestation of the church with the Department of Evangelism of the Division of Homeland Ministries. The only Asian on the general staff of the church is in the Division of Overseas Ministries and works one-half time for another denomination. An Asian-American who serves in a regional capacity is a Korean pastor working one-quarter time in the Pacific Southwest developing Asian ministries.

A recent consultation on Asian ministries among Disciples agreed that during the 1990s there will be a concentration on expansion of congregations among the Korean communities.[65] There are currently Korean congregations under development in Chicago, Los Angeles, Nashville, and Northern California. They have come to the United States as Protestant Christians, have experienced a United Church in Korea, and are attracted to the Disciples. The goal adopted was fifty new congregations during the decade. Ten of these will be initiated by regions, and the general church with direct help and financial support. Another forty will develop as "adopted" or "nesting" congregations in Anglo buildings. The latter, it is expected, will come to the Disciples for counsel, oversight, and support and should be received. It is important that they have pastors who are ordained or licensed while continuing their education.

The Consultation on Asian Ministries also pointed out the need for ministerial leadership among immigrant congregations and asked for a mentoring program for their pastors and for internships in Asian-American settings for Asian students in seminaries. The Consultation also noted the prevalence of bivocational ministry. It requested that three to five new pastors/students be recruited for training within the next eighteen months.

During the 1989-90 academic year, only two Asian-Americans Disciples were enrolled in a Master of Divinity degree program, both at McCormick Theological Seminary in Chicago where there is an

Asian community and opportunities for employment in Korean congregations. One doctoral student (Korean) is enrolled at the University of Chicago.

The Department of Ministry administers a small but growing Kagiwada Memorial Fund to help Asian Disciples preparing for ministry. It has assisted one or two students each of the past two years with grants of $500 to $750. The need for increased financial support of ministerial education is obvious if the goals of new Korean congregations are to be realized. That education should include participation in a Disciples community where these new Disciples can experience relationships among other Disciples.

Recommendations

1. How can the church determine whether it can meet the challenges of increasing ethnic diversity through the greater utilization of alternative pools of talent? A couple of studies offer insight into this question. One study conducted by Lexington Theological Seminary indicated that the personal qualities of a strong minister include: integrity, compassion, ability to work with people, self-confidence, a passion for hard work, and taking theological competence seriously. In addition to a deep personal faith, an interest in social issues and an awareness of forces that shape society are also important factors. A second study conducted by the University of Southern California found that people look for and admire the following characteristics among their leaders: honesty, competence, forward-looking vision, and inspiration. It is important to note that the lists of qualities from the two studies stress personal qualities and not technical competence, as the key indicators of leadership potential.

The studies would seem to indicate that the church may need to look beyond rigid criteria and more carefully consider ways of identifying, developing and supporting "non-traditional" candidates into ministry. For example, how do we determine if the newly immigrated young pastor is capable of leading a congregation in the US? What if the individual had led an effective ministry before coming to the US? Is it more advantageous to disrupt active ministry by forcing such a person into the structure of the seminary system? Is it possible to construct an alternate career path that would allow the "feeding of the sheep" not to be disrupted by the "pursuit of the sheepskin"?

    a. If personal qualities are indeed the most important leadership characteristics, would the church not be better served if persons possessing such qualities were "facilitated" into ministry within a more flexible and responsive training and development system? This presents a special challenge to those Disciples schools (colleges and especially seminaries) located in states with large ethnic populations.

b. In the secular world, personal assessment technology has flourished and could be useful in identifying future ministerial talent. It might be that the church is bypassing important talent pools which, with proper support, may help meet the needs of communities that are not currently being served. We recommend that regional commissions on ministry and seminaries consider the viability of these assessment tools in developing and identifying ethnic persons with ministerial talents.

c. Can a network of support be fashioned so that the "non-traditional" minister can receive the coaching and guidance he or she needs in the field? We recommend that regional commissions on ministry and seminaries begin the development of non-traditional education and training programs that will take into account the realities of language, e.g. Korean, French, Spanish; the time constraints of a bivocational minister; and the social context of the ethnic congregation.

2. We urge the Division of Higher Education to establish a desk to work exclusively with racial/ethnic minority issues. The main tasks of this person will be to assist the Division in the work of interpreting minority concerns, needs, and realities to churches, Disciples seminaries and colleges so as to help in the recruitment of African-American, Asian-American, and Hispanic students for ministry.

3. The standing of bivocational ministers must be clarified and elevated among the Disciples if the potential for ministry among these three groups is to be realized. Ministry begins with a sense of the call to ministry. How can that call be recognized and given status apart from the level of education of the candidate? This issue needs to be addressed throughout our denomination. Leadership must be taken by the Department of Ministry working with regional commissions, especially in those areas with a concentration of ethnic ministers. We recommend that the present *Policies and Criteria for the Order Ministry* in use by the Disciples be reviewed and revised.

4. Ministry among the growing number new of Asian and Hispanic-Americans can best be accomplished by persons who themselves are newcomers to the US. Their training must include experi-

ences with other Christians, especially faculty, who are bi-cultural and who have shown the capacity to live creatively in their native culture and in the US.

5. Education of ministers among racial/ethnic groups must be largely within a Disciples context if they are to take on a Disciples identity and continue in fellowship with the denomination. All Disciples colleges, universities, and seminaries must be staffed with African, Asian, and Hispanic-American faculty who can model, with integrity, survival in a multicultural environment. This calls for active recruitment of ethnic faculty who will develop curriculum relevant to ethnic ministries for Disciples schools. We further recommend the use of faculty from Latin America and the Caribbean as visiting professors to teach at both undergraduate and graduate schools.

6. The need for increased financial aid for racial/ethnic minority students considering ministry, or already in seminary, must be addressed with new realism. We have not attempted to compile a complete report of the resources now available or the amount needed if the Disciples are to achieve the goals of the decade. The Division of Higher Education or the Department of Ministry needs to catalogue all the present sources of financial aid from colleges, seminaries, regions, and foundations that are targeted for minorities. This information must be made available not only to assist those who counsel prospective ministers but to all ethnic congregations as well.

6

Disciples Women in Ministry

Given the task of addressing the situation of Disciples women serving as pastors in congregations, we began by assessing reasons for lack of gender inclusiveness in Disciples ministerial employment and concluded with recommendations for strategies to bring balance to pastoral positions. The direction which we undertook explored two areas: the seminary and the church.

Questions were posed to seminaries about preparation and graduation of women students in the decade from 1979 to 1989:

1. How many women completed degree programs?
2. Who were the women and what degree programs were completed?
3. What were the cumulative grade point averages for all students and for women?

Questions were posed to the church through regional ministers about present relocation practices:

1. How many women are serving in local congregations?
2. Have specific steps been initiated to encourage congregations to call women?
3. What have you done in search processes to encourage congregations to call women?
4. In the decade from 1979 through 1989, how many congregations have called women to full-time positions? To full-time interim positions?

This exploration led us to more questions which are presented later in this chapter in the summary of our research representing the need for ongoing dialogue.

The Situation

Three approaches were followed to assess the situation for women in ministry in the Christian Church (Disciples of Christ): theological, historical, and structural.

The biblical ground for inclusion of women as carriers of the gospel can be substantiated. It was noted that biblical stories, such as the "woman at the well" (John 4: 7-29) and the resurrection narrative in Mark (16:7), demonstrate the inclusion of women throughout the work and life of Jesus as messengers of his identity and of the good news of his life-giving presence. Paul arrived at the position that all Christians are equal as members of the body of Christ (Gal 3:28).

Historically, Disciples women have served as pastors since the mid-to-late 1880s. Between 1880 and 1893 biblical scholars, denominational leaders, and journal editors debated the theology of women in ministry in denominational publications, *The Christian Standard* and *The Christian Evangelist*. The opposition to women in ministry was significant. Although modern scholarship has enhanced biblical understanding and interpretation, the acceptance of ordained women has not kept pace with developing theological insights.

Most early Disciples leaders, including Barton Warren Stone and Alexander Campbell, resisted women responding to God's call as ordained preachers and pastors. A large proportion of today's church leadership (general, regional, academic, and editorial) supports the movement for women, and yet the battle is not won.

Today a large number of Disciples women have completed Master of Divinity degrees and additional theological studies. They are comparable to their male counterparts in gifts, graces, and abilities for ministry and are shown to be stronger academic performers than the men.[66]

While scholarly achievements and historical understandings toward the situation of women in ministry have improved, those insights seem to remain in the realms of theory. Church polity is based on practices which, over time, become traditional, externally imposed forms of governance. These practices are employed by congregations to make their lives more vital, meaningful, and acceptable. Frequently they become that which determines "life" rather than serving to evoke life-giving "new" forms. Because most assumed structures imply "keeping control over" organizations, they perpetuate what "has been," and what "has been" is a male-dominated leadership team including clergy.

Procedures

A questionnaire was sent to the following seminaries asking for data related to women graduates between the years of 1979 and 1989: Brite Divinity School, Texas Christian University; Lexington Theological Seminary, Disciples Seminary Foundation, School of Theology at Claremont; Disciples Divinity House, University of Chicago; and Disciples Divinity House, Vanderbilt University. The same information was gathered by members of the team for Christian Theological Seminary and Phillips Graduate Seminary. Due to changes in record keeping procedures, not all schools were able to respond with comparable data in time for the completion of this research. Table I shows the compilation of received responses.

Table I

Women Seminary Graduates 1979-1989

Brite Divinity School

Women Graduates

1979	1980	1981	1982	1983	1984	1985	1986	1987	1988	1989	Total
9	3	7	4	4	12	9	16	8	9	8	89

Degrees Conferred

M.Div.	MRE	MTh	MTS	D.Min.	Total
77	7	2	1	1	88

Cumulative GPA	1986	1987	1988	1989
All students	3.463	3.393	3.410	3.396
Women students	3.530	3.714	3.652	3.549

University of Chicago Divinity School, Disciples Divinity House

Women Graduates

1979	1980	1981	1982	1983	1984	1985	1986	1987	1988	1989	Total
0	0	1	2	2	1	1	2	1	3	3	16

Degrees Conferred

M.Div.	MA	PhD	Total
2	10	4	16

Phillips Graduate Seminary

Cumulative GPA

	1979	1980	1981	1982	1983	1984	1985	1986	1987	1988	1989
Women	3.63	2.79	3.53	3.34	3.40	3.15	3.53	3.45	3.25	3.34	3.39
Men	3.21	3.00	3.48	3.01	2.99	3.50	3.00	3.00	3.30	3.41	3.31

98 *Discerning the Call*

Table I

(Continued from previous page)

Vanderbilt University Divinity School, Disciples Divinity House

Women Graduates

1979	1980	1981	1982	1983	1984	1985	1986	1987	1988	1989	Total
0	0	1	2	4	3	0	0	6	2	5	23

12 remain in process in 1989 for a total of 35

Degrees Conferred
M.Div. M.Div./JD
22   1

Degrees in Process
M.Div. MTS Total
10   2   35

Totals of Degrees Conferred

M.Div.	MRE	MTh	MTS	D.Min.	JD	MA	PhD	Total
122	7	2	3	2	1	10	4	151

From statistics prepared for the *Fact Book on Theological Education, 1987-88*, the following observations were drawn (specifically for the M.Div. and in-sequence D.Min. programs): Between 1976 and 1987 there was a slight decline in male enrollees for these two degree programs while in that ten year period total seminary enrollments rose thirty percent. Total enrollment in the pre-ordination programs rose only 8.6%. The enrollment of women, however, in those two programs increased 110%. The year 1987 marks the third year of a decline in absolute numbers of male enrollment. This means that since 1976, the growth in these two programs had been entirely among women, whose percentage rose from 11.5% to 22.4%. It was further reported that in just ten years (since 1976-77) female M.Div. recipients had increased 224% (from 462 to 1,496). In that same time period male M.Div. graduates rose by only 4.6% (from 5,158 to 5,394). Since this statement reflects all seminaries, the need to question the employment of the increased number of women graduates was confirmed.[67]

The Yearbook and Directory of the Christian Church (Disciples of Christ), 1989, was studied to determine the current status of the graduates from the designated decade.

Table II
1989 Areas of Service for Women Graduates 1979-1989
from Five Disciples Seminaries

Arena of Ministry	Brite Divinity School	Christian Theological Seminary	Phillips Graduate Seminary	Chicago Divinity House	Vanderbilt Divinity House
Pastor	23	15	19	2	2
Assoc. Pastor	24	6	(above)	0	2
Christian Education	1	1	1	0	1
Missionary	1	0	0	0	1
Chaplain	3	5	5	0	1
Higher Education	0	2	1	2	1
Campus Ministry	1	0	0	0	1
Regional Staff	0.5	2	3	1	0
General Staff	2	1	0	0	0
Other	25.5	7	11	2	2
Advanced Study	3	2	1	0	3
No Standing	0	3	0	9	9
Deceased	0	2	0	0	0
Totals	84	46	41	16	23

Total Graduates   210

Distribution of Employment

Local Congregation	41%
Regional/General Staff	4%
Other (includes no standing)	21%
Higher Education	2%
Chaplaincy	6%
Advanced Study	4%

Region Survey Status of Women in Ministry

A survey instrument was distributed to regional ministers to assist in determining present relocation practices and results in the various regions. Of 36 surveys distributed, seventeen were returned.

1. How many full time pastoral positions are there in your region? <u>1376</u>
2. How many women are serving in local congregations in your region? <u>265</u>

    <u>93</u> Pastors (single staff)

    <u>14</u> Senior pastor (multiple staff)

    <u>19</u> Co-pastors

    <u>78</u> Associate pastors

    <u>10</u> Assistant pastors

    <u>11</u> Youth pastors

    <u>7</u> Music ministers

    <u>20</u> Directors of Christian education

    <u>4</u> Student pastors

    <u>9</u> Student associate pastors

3. How many clergy couples are serving in your region? <u>109</u>

    In what capacities?

    <u>18</u> Co-pastors

    <u>8</u> Pastor and assistant

    <u>7</u> Regional ministry

    <u>4</u> Each pastor of one congregation

    <u>15</u> Specialized ministry (Many didn't get named)

4. How many women are serving in non-parish settings? <u>91</u>
5. Have any specific steps (educational events, resolutions, etc.) been initiated to encourage the calling of women to congregations? <u>Yes</u>

    Please describe:

    Regions named a number of steps, including advocacy in search processes (12), literature to congregations (5), and assembly resolutions (6).

Disciples Women in Ministry 101

6. What have you done to encourage congregations in the search process to call women?

    This question, much like #5, continued the listing of such steps as those named there. Other such steps as intentionally asking search committees to interview women (10 regions) and taking an ordained woman to a meeting with the search committee (1 region).

7. Have any women from your region gone into the ministry? <u>59</u>

8. How many people are on regional commissions on the ministry? <u>216</u>

    How many clergywomen? <u>37</u>

9. In the past ten years how many of your congregations have issued calls to clergywomen for full-time positions:
    <u>200</u> First time (several regions said this number was not retrievable)
    <u>55</u> Second time
    <u>0</u> Other (no reliable way to gather this data)

10. How many congregations have called women to full-time interim positions? <u>54</u>

11. Is there a seminary in your region? <u>12 of the 17 said Yes</u>

12. Comments: no additional comments were offered.

Conclusions

- The statistics describe the situation: there is an increasing number of qualified women candidates for various church positions. Why they are not called to those positions is an intangible factor or composite of factors. Even though scripture supports women as leaders/ministers, tradition and culture play stronger roles than skills and abilities in the determinations of placement.

- The information gathered from those seminaries that reveal grade point averages (see Table I) illustrates that women are consistently higher achievers academically. It seems apparent, therefore, that academic achievement is not used as a criterion of call by local search committees.

- Table II demonstrates that 41% of the 210 graduates from the recent decade are serving local congregations. If general staff, higher education, and chaplaincy are included the figure reaches 55% of women graduates who are in occupations related to the church. Table I shows that 84% of the decade's women graduates were prepared for service in the local church.

- The questions, then, turn toward opportunities available to the women and men for fulfilling their calls. Currently just under fifteen percent of the full-time positions are held by women. Slightly less than half of those positions are as senior pastor or single staff. The Christian Church (Disciples of Christ) needs to be far more intentional in encouraging and enabling congregations to receive and give opportunity to ALL persons called to ministry.

There is need for a specifically designed educational program about women in ministry. The evidence shows that few unique methods are being undertaken by regions to enhance this cause. Such efforts as one region's practice of having an ordained woman meet with search committees are too few and far between.

There is evidence to demonstrate that the most successful regions in the relocation of women into pastorates are regions whose regional ministers have been in office more than six or seven years. Is this because, when they go to congregations for the second time, or subsequently, to aid in the search process, there has been enough trust established to do more effective advocacy for women?

The church needs to see specific data about the future of ministry. If as many ministers are retiring as projected, what does this say about the church in the year 2003? Will one-quarter, one-half, or one-third of the available clergy be women? Such information can help those who are seeking to bring change now. Regional ministers and commissions on ministry need to be informed of these data, as they are sources of help in discerning the best ways to go about changing the picture.

Summary Questions

As noted in the introductory remarks, the team moved from questions to more questions. While the latter are not directly related to the status of women, they do seem pertinent to the issue of seeking quality ordained leadership for the church in the twenty-first century. The questions are directed toward the two foci of the team's work: the seminary and the church. The team proposes these questions with the hope that they will stimulate thinking in some new directions.

"New" questions for seminaries:
1. Does survival of the educational institution dictate a "marketing mode" of education? For example, a curriculum designed around "block courses" is offered at the Tulsa campus of Phillips Graduate Seminary one day a week. This provides second-career students, who also may need to support families, a professional degree program and allows for full time employment.
    a. Does formation (of ministers) happen only in class?
    b. Is the "work schedule" a primary consideration in educational requirements for degree programs?
2. Are criteria for seminary admissions at cross-purposes with criteria for successful ministry?
    a. Is there a difference between recruiting students and enlisting ministerial candidates?
    b. Is *call* considered in recruiting students? Is it a "soft" call or a "hard" call? For example, will the student willingly make sacrifices to complete the response to the call?
3. Are seminaries leader-preparation oriented or are they scholastic centers?
    a. What is the proportion of students not considering parish ministry?
    b. What is the proportion of students without church experience in their background?
    c. Are there more potential ministerial candidates than there are available positions?
4. What is an "inclusive institution?" For example, has the institution established a setting in which female and male are substantially included rather than one which plugs in faces in a quasi-quota fashion?
5. Are seminaries accountable to the church?
    a. Do seminary boards have representation from the church?
    b. Do seminary boards have direction-setting power?
    c. Does lack of financial support from the church (Basic Mission Finance represents only 6-8% of operational support) indicate lack of relationship, hence, lack of need for accountability?

"New" questions for the church:
1. Does the church educate for and enlist to ministry?
    a. Who asks: "Young woman/man, have you considered ministry?"

104   *Discerning the Call*

   b. Is there available funding for required vocational-direction testing?
2. Is there a possibility that the practicing parish clergy is becoming "feminized?"
   a. Is a factor low salaries for ministers?
   b. Is a factor the preponderance of small congregations?
3. Should the church impose qualifications and requirements for ordination beyond seminary education? For instance, a post-seminary time of three to five years in the profession and under care to allow for assessment of the following before ordination?
   a. Relational skills, including the practical
   b. Administrative skill, including the practical
   c. Allow the candidate to establish church relationships and become KNOWN.

Recommendations

1. Realizing that historical and cultural barriers inhibit the calling of women to positions of authority (e.g. general, regional, and senior minister of multiple staff congregations), it is recommended that programs exploring those barriers be implemented. Plans for such implementation may be 1994 Quadrennial "workshops," CWF study series, Laywomen-Clergywomen Conversations, and regional assemblies.
2. Regions should be encouraged to establish specific programs aimed at educating congregations through experience about the pastoral leadership abilities of women. Such programs may include women as interim ministers or pulpit supply and women as retreat keynoters or assembly speakers.
3. The Conference of Regional Ministers and Moderators should begin a process of *advocating* for women in relocation by insisting that their files be given serious consideration in all searches.
4. Regional commissions on ministry need to give serious consideration to procedures for receiving candidates seeking transfers of standing from other denominations. A carefully scrutinized process for persons transferring to the Christian Church (Disciples of Christ) from other denominations will help protect potential calls for Disciples women.
5. Regions in coordination with the Department of Ministry should monitor salary and benefits for women in ministry to determine variances in parity between female and male pastors.

7

Characteristics for Success

Do we know what kind of people ought to be Disciples ministers? Do we know how to recruit and train them for that task? To what extent are we succeeding in attracting them to ministry and preparing them to provide it? How are those variables changing over recent years? Are there things we could be doing to increase the magnitude and quality of the flow of committed ministerial candidates?

These are the questions we were asked to research, and to which we found surprisingly clear and usable answers. We do know what kind of people do well in ministry, but we are not doing well in recruiting them and nurturing them through the rough early years in clerical life. We seem to be losing a little ground in the competition with other professions for the brightest candidates, but otherwise we are getting about the same group of people we always have. And considering how little we have been doing in recent decades, it is not surprising we have been outcompeted. There is much that could be done, and a great deal of it is known.

To address the issue of ministerial enlistment, the following strategy is recommended: (1) that the church adopt and implement a church-wide priority of the identification, recruitment, support, and training of promising ministerial candidates beginning no later than junior high school and extending through the first five years of ministry; and that (2) the church intentionally reformulate a vision of the ministerial office, focusing on the basic nurturing and educational functions of ministry within an essentially missionary North American setting, and that (3) seminary and other ministerial training increasingly focus on the development of communication abilities and the spiritual nurture of the candidate.

The three prongs of this strategy will be treated *seriatim*, though there is considerable overlap. Supporting data underlying the conclusions will be included in the discussion of the appropriate theme.

A Churchwide Enlistment and Nurturing Strategy

We know who should be ministers. The research from several schools, denominations, and regions consistently clusters on these characteristics as differentiating excellent ministers from those less highly regarded (by a wide range of raters, who are surprisingly similar in their selections). These desirable characteritics for ministers may be identified by self or by others:

1. High (but not rare) intellectual ability, as measured by seminary grade point average.
2. High self-esteem and self-acceptance.
3. Open, affirming, flexible relational style that produces effective communication.
4. Ability to nurture faith in laity.
5. Ability to handle conflict, accept differences, and admit weaknesses.
6. Commitment to the faith and the church.
7. Demonstrated ability to care for individuals and the broader community.
8. Willingness to serve without claiming the deference or appreciation of others.
9. Responsibility in task fulfillment.
10. Ability to accept opposition without retaliation or discouragement.
11. Commitment to recruiting and training laity in specific aspects of mission.

These personal characteristics seem to be the crucial determining variables for effectiveness in Christian ministry, but do not appear adequately emphasized in seminary recruitment or curricula. The church should intentionally seek people with these personal characteristics, and/or design a guidance system for seminary and pre-seminary students that further develops them.

Though the basic personality profile of persons entering seminary seems to be fairly constant and appropriate over recent decades, there are major changes in other attributes—some positive, some negative.

— There is a gradual decline in cognitive ability of candidates over the last twenty-five years. In the late 1940s, 3.9% of Phi Beta Kappas entered seminary. In the early 1980s, that figure was down to 0.8%.

— There is a major shift in demographics of entering students. Almost one-half now are women, and the majority of both genders are second career. An increasing number are racial/ethnic minorities.

— There is a decline in the percentage of candidates with a broad-based liberal education, with pre-seminary study in religion, philosophy, and the humanities.

— There is a decline in the percentage of candidates who were nurtured in the church throughout their pre-seminary years, resulting in the need for more basic religious education at the seminary level.

— Women seminarians demonstrate better cognitive abilities on intelligence tests and record higher seminary grade point averages, but declare less interest in parish ministry. That appears to be related to their expectation that there will be less opportunity for them to be hired and to advance in parishes. The poorest academic and personal qualifications are consistently demonstrated by older white male students, who have the highest motivation for work in the parish.

There are some definite implications to these qualities and changes:

— Knowing what kind of persons become quality ministers, we should develop programs to enable identification of these persons, where possible from early adolescence, and to awaken in them an interest in ministry from that point. Local clergy and church camps should be crucial elements, so scholarships to camps and training events should be instituted. Testing should be done prior to seminary. Enlistment should not be left to seminary recruiters but should be a whole church effort. Emphasis on development and utilization of test instruments that measure interpersonal and leadership abilities should be increased. These are properly functions that fall to the oversight of the general manifestation of the church.

— Once persons have declared an interest in ministry, there should be an intentional, consistent process of moving those with excellent potential into preaching positions by mid-seminary. This may involve a significant change in seminary field education programs including standardized salaries, limits on hours of work, and excellence in supervision. There should specifically be an intentional position taken on equipping our highly qualified female and racial/ethnic minority candidates.

— To facilitate the changes discussed above, we strongly recommend a general church effort to redesign and revise procedures to assist regional commissions on ministry. Wide variations in commission practices from region to region appear to make it possible for poorly qualified persons to enter Disciples ministry from other denominations, then to move freely within it. In many cases this influx makes it more difficult for our more promising women ministers to find positions.

Revisioning the Ministerial Office

There is a major structural problem in American Protestantism in general and in the office of ministry in particular that works against clergy morale, widens the clergy-laity gap, and interferes with enlistment. Incentives that attracted young Christians into ministry twenty-five years ago are much less available, leading to halfhearted recruitment efforts and disillusionment in newly ordained clergy. Some of the major factors in that difficulty are the following:

— Clergy job satisfaction is considerably lower than twenty-five years ago, reflecting in part the failure of congregations to reward ministers for the performance of the basic theological tasks.

— Little authority is granted to the office of minister within contemporary congregations. Witness the large number of clergy firings and the difficulty of achieving adequate compensation.

— Disciples are afflicted by a larger clergy-laity gap, in terms of social, political, and religious attitudes, than are most other Protestant denominations (and it's quite large in most). Current research indicates that many people who drop out of church altogether are most like the clergy who lead their congregations. This interferes markedly with the ability of these clergy and laity to enjoy each other and suggests that identifying clergy personnel and ecclesiastical structures to link those inclined to leave existing congregations and the clergy most likely to interest them would be helpful. Perhaps new congregational establishment should particularly target these potential or recent dropouts.

— Responding in part to (and contributing to the widening of) this gap, clergy are increasingly unlikely to engage congregations in serious ethical and theological reflection. Studies throughout the last twenty-five years have identified the fact that Christians find little help in thinking through ethical questions from their congregations. Research demonstrates that clergy are least likely to speak out on ethical/theological issues on which they perceive a major difference between themselves and the laity, and are especially unlikely to lead laity through the process by which they themselves came to the conclusions that currently guide their thought. As a result, laity are not being equipped with the methodology for theological and ethical reflection—which in turn further alienates them from a clergy that has reached its conclusions of the basis of such reflection.

— Due to the width of the gap, and the disinclination of clergy to either teach the methods by which faithful decisions are reached or disagree with their congregations' known positions, there is a tendency to preach a gospel trimmed down to fit the level of spiritual and religious interests of the congregation.

— There has been a retreat from what Clark Williamson[68] identified as the one indispensable function of religious faith, "that it help people to understand what it means to be human in the light of ultimate reality," and that it equip them to live out the implications of that understanding. Since most of the dropouts are those that believe more rather than less like the leadership of the church, and since research indicates that the number of people who leave because the church is too liberal is roughly balanced by the number of people who leave because it is too conservative, it appears that the net loss primarily represents people who are bored by the church's refusal to preach a gospel demanding enough to be worthy of their attention.

The Christian Church (Disciples of Christ) needs to make a significant effort to create a new vision of the ministerial office, focusing on its nurturing and educational functions. It needs to teach both the content of the Christian faith and the process the church has traditionally used to arrive at decisions, and to make the invitation to provide such teaching central in the recruitment of potential clergy.

To enable clergy to focus on these teaching and nurturing functions, the church must identify means to more widely share the administrative functions that occupy a high percentage of clergy time today. Clergy need to be freed to be their congregations' primary teachers, and need not be expended in the administrative efforts at which they are not particularly skilled. To enable that, some other group of Christians needs to be equipped and positioned to handle major administrative responsibilities.

Because of the absence of the tools for theological and ethical discussion among the laity and the broader populace, ministerial enlistment and training should emphasize that the church is now in a missionary position in North America. There is an excitement and an element of adventure involved in taking the gospel into territory in which it is little known, and emphasizing that aspect in enlistment efforts may invite those with the skills actually needed in an increasingly multicultural situation.

Revision of Ministerial Formation

We know the personal qualities, the technical skills, and the vision of the church and world that we need in ministry. But we spend a disproportionate share of our resources in ministerial education in ways that do not directly impact the variables identified as crucial: high self-esteem, communication skills, conflict management, spiritual depth, a teaching methodology.

Hence a final and emphatic recommendation: Seminary education, pre-seminary and post-seminary education, and seminary extracurricular life should increasingly focus on the development of conflict-management skills, the continued development of (hopefully already very good) communication skills, and the spiritual nurture of the candidate. This may involve a reallocation of resources away from some traditional academic fields, or a rearrangement of emphases within them; or the development of corollary requirements and programs in the manner of field education at many seminaries. This is a responsibility of the ordaining bodies, ultimately, and should not remain isolated as a solely seminary responsibility.

Afterword

A year of research and writing by seven study teams culminated in a period of evaluation and reflection by those who were invited to attend a three-day planning conference October 1-3, 1990 in Indianapolis. Time was given for serious consideration of the first seven chapters of this book, as it was distributed, in draft form, two months prior to the conference to the thirty-seven participants.[69] Important questions on content, philosophy, and style were raised, and appreciation was expressed for the process of the study and for the recommendations that emerged. It is now a matter of testing the conclusions of the study teams and the planning conference to see if the church is prepared to implement the recommendations that are offered. Some recommendations are general, some specific. Some recommendations have barbs, some are modest. All have a perspective that represents who we are as a church and a potential for improving the way we function.

Interestingly the majority of suggestions offered for advancing the means by which ministerial enlistment, nurture, and support take shape are low-cost or no-cost items. The immediate call is for rethinking our existing processes and procedures rather than creating new programs. It was concluded that the critical word for the church in ministerial enlistment is "coordination." Coordination among general units, regions, educational institutions, and congregations is dependent upon cooperation, and that must be intentional.

Two central themes recur throughout this study which confirm our initial assumptions and deserve to be noted. **First, pastors are significant models for ministry and the primary sources of invitation for candidacy into ministry.** These may be influential clergy with whom people come into contact at camps and conferences, on campuses, or in the ecumenical arena as well as "home church" pastors. **Secondly, youth work is crucial not only for enlistment to ministry but for the health of the church as well.** Those youth and young adults who may have a strong commitment to the gospel and a desire to participate in the church, but do not have an inclination toward ordained ministry, also need to be nurtured for the gifts they bring to church involvement and leadership.

This volume points to the possibilities for the design of an enlistment to ministry/support of ministry effort that can be broadly accepted throughout the Christian Church (Disciples of Christ). Intended for use by the whole church, certain recommendations can be customized to fit the specific needs of regions, congregations, and educational institutions. At the same time, this volume identifies problems that must be faced if such efforts "to advance the quality" are to have integrity.

Having lived with this project for two years, it is apparent to us that some of the early assumptions, if not incorrect, were incomplete. We also recognize that the project and these contents, regardless of how carefully prepared, have omissions which can impede an effective approach to a comprehensive understanding of the church's ministry. The purpose of this afterword, in part, is to identify some of those omissions so they can be added to the thinking process.

Elitism

Without proper definition, "advancing the quality" can imply an elitist attitude in regard to ministerial characteristics. As with many charged words, elite may unnecessarily carry a negative connotation. If elite means choice or select, such a ministry is desirable. The church deserves clergy who are spiritually disciplined, well educated, oriented to Christian values, emotionally stable, and competent to perform ministerial tasks. The acceptance of mediocrity in many areas of human life is an unfortunate tendency that must be overcome. Strength in ministry as an ideal is part of our Christian heritage and is certainly affirmed through the Campbellian tradition.

The Christian Church (Disciples of Christ) lacks a "theology of ministry," indeed the term appears nowhere else in this book but here. Without a specific notion of ministry that the church can accept, we will continue to struggle to understand the functions of the ministerial office. The suggestion of a "spiritually empowered practical theologian" is a step in the direction of clarifying ways in which the church sees its ministers. Yet it also is problematic, for no one word or phrase can adequately capture the essence of Christian leadership. If asked whether spiritually empowered practical theologian is meant to be definitive or descriptive, the answer certainly must be descriptive. Were such a theology to emerge it must include Christ-centered identity, discerning the call, the art of critical thinking, and the importance of worship as a doxological and community-forming activity.

Long disregarded is the church's recognition of bivocational ministers, without whom some congregations would cease to function. While many bivocational ministers have the right of ministerial standing through the category of "licenses lay preachers" in the *Policies and Criteria for the Order of Ministry*, these policies concentrate on the full-time, ordained minister.[70] Educational opportunities generally have not been designed for the circumstances of bivocational ministers since they do not have freedom to attend regular classes during the week or extended classes on week-ends. Programs, such as those offered by the Missouri School of Religion, attempt to take into account the need for non-traditional course offerings in non-traditional settings.[71]

Ecumenics

The legacy of the Stone/Campbell Movement has provided Disciples a strong commitment to Christian unity. With unity as our vision, we have been careful not to be exclusive. This strength has perhaps also been our weakness. In order to avoid building walls, we have neglected to erect even guideposts. As a result, we find it difficult to measure, evaluate, and even articulate our own positions. Disciples must realize that we have significant contributions to offer the ecumenical community, especially with regard to presence at the table and proclamation of the word.

This book does not address our participation in the Consultation on Church Union. In partnership for almost thirty years, Disciples have influenced and been influenced by discussions of cooperative approaches to ministry. We need to be conscious of appropriate responses to the eight other denominations in COCU while maintaining the values that make our own concepts of ministry distinctive.[72]

No discussion of ministry can be complete without reference to the Disciples-UCC "Ecumenical Partnership." Regardless of what formal action the 1993 St. Louis joint meeting of the General Assembly and the General Synod approves, ministry is clearly part of our future in terms of mutual recognition and reconciliation. As our discussions with the UCCs proceed, attention to this area will demand particular care. It also may afford the greatest possibilities for "advancing the quality."

Culture

The church has long known that North American society is becoming increasingly multicultural but has not known precisely how to engage this change. Beyond attempts at tokenism or quotas, pulpits, pews, classrooms, faculties, and staffs reflect the Anglo majority which makes up the bulk of its membership. In some parts of the United States and Canada that majority has fast become a minority so the predominant styles of worship and ecclesial organization that existed are becoming a memory, even though they continue to prevail as the conceptual norm. Study materials, hymnals, curricula, and other church resources are still written in English with western European images. In addition, there are pockets in the United States in which the Christian community, regardless of its ethnic or cultural orientation, is becoming a minority through the growth of non-Christian traditions which adds yet another dimension to our Christian experiences.

A key to the church in the 1990s and on into the twenty-first century is *cultural flexibility* relative to ecclesiology, sociology, and education. One deficiency, particularly of United States citizens, is our comfort in being verbally and mentally monolingual. In a rapidly emerging multicultural environment, merely expressing Anglo theology in Spanish, Korean, Chinese, or even Hindi does not make the church inclusive. Christians are uniquely called to give leadership to the whole of society, and that means that ministers must be prepared to respond to this multicultural reality.

Cultural flexibility also means that new immigrant populations as well as settled populations must be recognized. This is difficult for we tend to acknowledge only those cultures which are most visibly present or with whom we have had historical connections such as Blacks, Hispanics, and Asians. Sub-cultures have been lumped together based on commonness of language or color when, indeed, they are quite distinct. Native Americans and Haitians are but two groups that have been overlooked, due in part to their isolation from the mainstream of church life.

Ministry

A primary issue with which the church must contend is its diminishing influence in modern society. Certainly there are signs of renewed interest in church life and indications of growth. Reports show that church crib rooms and nurseries are beginning to swell, which has to be encouraging to pastors. However we have enjoyed growth swells before so there must be concern about the church's ability to offer a continuity of spiritual depth, educational substance, leadership opportunities, meaningful missions, and a community of support and fellowship in ways that keep people active and involved.

Vital ministerial leadership is the first line of interpretation and vision for the church. Poorly paid clergy with few offsetting rewards will quickly begin to question the value of their work and ultimately their calls. The perception of ministers by those they serve is an issue of esteem. Adequate compensation and other tangible support bases need to be sufficient not only to attract new people into ministry but to provide for those who are in ministry now.

Financial considerations are extremely important to recent seminary graduates, for educational indebtedness continues to mount. Conversations with seminarians reveal that they realize Christian ministry will not afford them a life of economic luxury, and they accept that. However, it is unconscionable that ministers should enter their first full-time positions carrying as much as $25,000 in undergraduate and graduate loan obligations resulting from seven to eight years of academic study with minimal income to effect a non-burdening repayment schedule. Expanded and new financial aids resources must be developed to correct this situation.

Another element of ministerial esteem is ongoing education. Standard educational requirements have been established for entry into full-time Christian ministry without much attention given to outlets for spiritual and intellectual growth beyond basic seminary studies. Continuing education events are necessary to help ministers maintain freshness thereby reducing burn-out. Too often continuing education leaves are based on convenience of time and locale. Ministers and congregations together must carefully plan and protect opportunities for professional enhancement and personal enrichment from intrusions by last minute schedule changes.

Collegiality is critical to maintaining enthusiasm and energy for ministry. Learning can occur through private study and reflection, of course, but it is more effective in a collegial environment. The refinement of ideas through sharing and testing in groups is a learning mechanism as important for settled clergy as the classroom is for seminarians. Many people talk to the ministers; to whom does the minister talk? The concept of mentor should be expanded beyond the traditional supervising-minister/student-minister model.

Conclusion

Much has been accomplished in this project thus far. The study teams have collected significant data and proposed provocative recommendations. Those who attended the planning conference offered insightful suggestions for implementing strategies to strengthen the church's ministry. Each participant in this project represents important constituent groups, disciplines, careers, and interests. All have the capability to make a difference in the arenas in which they live and work, and the dividends of their activities are apparent already. As this information continues to broaden, more Disciples will become conscious of the need to support Christian ministry in new ways.

A wealth of material could have been included in this book, as readers may observe much has been left unsaid. The results of this research phase of the project are not meant to be comprehensive but stimulating. Simply producing sufficient numbers of candidates to fill slots in seminaries or pulpits is not our goal. The broader purpose is to discover ways in which capable individuals can discern the call to Christian ministry and ways in which the church can discern the qualities it desires in its ministerial leadership.

There is no indication that members of the Christian Church (Disciples of Christ) are disinterested in the nature of its ministry. Rather, we seem to assume the position that ministry will take care of itself. The twelve year priority adopted by the 1987 Louisville General Assembly of *developing vital congregations as dynamic faith communities in prophetic, redemptive and reconciling ministries to the whole world* demands that there be effective leadership to give vision and encouragement to congregations. While this leadership may be expected to originate with the professional ministry, it is ultimately a responsibility of the total church.

The following summary of major findings offers an umbrella of ideas by which congregations, institutions, regions, and general units of the church can evaluate their practices and posture their futures. The challenge before us is to grapple with these ideas in relation to our existing or planned programs. Implicit recommendations are contained in this afterword, but this synopsis of recommendations, like the findings, is the amalgam of the seven study teams' proposals and suggests entry points by which we can pursue the goal of enhancing the church's ministerial leadership.

Findings and Recommendations

FINDING

It has been clearly demonstrated through this study, as in other contemporary research, that a strong recruitment program for church-related colleges and universities and an effective enlistment program for Christian ministry cannot succeed without quality programs for junior high and high school youth. Regardless of inducements and mechanisms which seem to produce immediate results, personal attention to young people needs to be intentional and sustained. This is fundamental.

RECOMMENDATIONS

— *The church effectively affirm and cultivate a lively sense of spirituality within adolescents*

— *Interpretive materials be prepared to aid pastors, youth workers, and others enabling them to enlist persons for ministry*

— *The church give young people "tools" by which to discern and participate in God's work in the world*

— *The church spend time with youth where they are; in places, moments, and ways where youth culture is mediated*

—*Youth be involved directly in the church's ministry through such experiences as mission trips, leading worship, serving communion, teaching, and hospital visitation*

FINDING

A drawback to our current structure is the absence of a locus for coordination of ministerial issues. It is uncharacteristic of Disciples to create a central authority, so we have evolved numerous divisions, departments, commissions, and committees that carry ministry on their agendas. These have functioned adequately for the support of ministry, though such a disconnected system cannot achieve the desired inclusiveness.

RECOMMENDATIONS

—*A single office be created, or an existing one be designated by the General Board, to furnish oversight, from enlistment through retirement, for coordinating policy-making and review, developing*

> program materials, compiling comprehensive lists of probable ministerial candidates for enlistment and training in ministry, and assisting with relocation
>
> — *The church recognize and ritualize the place of Christian mentors, such as campus ministers, camp counselors, field education supervisors, and teachers*
>
> — *Visible support of those in ministry be enhanced, from the time they go to college until beyond their retirement*
>
> — *The church revitalize and renew its entire educational program as the proper context out of which to call young persons into full-time ministry*
>
> — *The "under care" programs of most regions be clarified and coordination across regional lines be initiated*
>
> — *More direct links be established between local churches and campus ministers*

FINDING

The expectations which the church has of its ministers have not changed significantly over the past twenty years. Although the manner in which persons approach the practice of ministry has changed dramatically, and the changes in society at large have been enormous. For example, the qualities of personal integrity, pastoral human relations skills, preaching and teaching abilities, theological competence, and an exhibited commitment to the gospel are still rated highly by search committees. These qualities also may be present in bivocational leadership, which has become the norm for many congregations.

RECOMMENDATIONS

> — *The concept of call to ministry as a gradual process be explored further and developed within congregational settings.*
>
> — *The church make a conscious effort to communicate a new vision of the ministerial office, focusing on its nurturing and educational function*
>
> — *Seminary education, pre-seminary and post-seminary education, and extracurricular educational life refocus on development of conflict-management skills, the continued development of communication skills, and the spiritual nurture of candidates*

— *The church look beyond rigid criteria for certification of ministers and carefully consider ways of identifying, developing, educating, and supporting "non-traditional" candidates into ministry*

— *Undergraduate schools and theological education institutions design instructional programs for bivocational ministers that will undergird their pastoral skills*

FINDING

Standards that the predominantly white church has seen as normative are not sufficiently appropriate for racial/ethnic minority congregations. Educational criteria and numbers of available clergy present distinct problems for racial/ethnic minorities in the selection of ministerial leadership. Role models for young persons are strong but few, and financial resources for education and for sustaining ministry are limited.

RECOMMENDATIONS

— *The standing of bivocational ministers be clarified among Disciples so that the potential for ministry among racial/ethnic groups can be realized*

— *Education for racial/ethnic ministers be largely within a Disciples context so that they can take on a Disciples identity and continue in fellowship with the denomination*

— *Every effort be made to staff Disciples colleges, universities, and seminaries with African, Asian, and Hispanic-American faculty who can model, with integrity, survival and success in a multicultural environment*

— *The need for increased financial aid for racial/ethnic minority students considering ministry or already in seminary be addressed with a new realism*

FINDING

Disciples can trace the ordination of women back over one hundred years, although women's roles frequently remain marginal to the church's leadership. The perception is that there is not a sufficient number of ministers available to serve congregations. This perception is faulty. The reality is that there is a reluctance to call women as single pastors or as senior ministers when they are ready to relocate beyond their first ministerial positions.

RECOMMENDATIONS

> —Regions establish specific, experience-based programs aimed at educating congregations about the pastoral leadership abilities of women
>
> —Regional commissions on ministry give serious attention to procedures for receiving candidates seeking transfers of standing from other denominations
>
> —Regions, in coordination with the Department of Ministry, monitor salaries and benefits for women in ministry to determine variances in parity between female and male pastors

Postscript

A selected bibliography of books and articles on ministry is appended for further reading. Survey instruments, questionnaires, and compilations of responses referenced throughout this book are available upon request from the Division of Higher Education, 11780 Borman Drive, Suite 100, St. Louis, Missouri 63146-4159; 314/991-3000.

Notes

[1] Janet A. Long, The Woman Pastor's Lot." *The Disciple*, (June 1990), p. 13. (Ms. Long currently serves as Senior Minister, Washington Avenue Christian Church, Elyria, Ohio)

[2] Brite Divinity School, Texas Christian University; Christian Theological Seminary; Lexington Theological Seminary; Phillips Graduate Seminary; Disciples Divinity House, University of Chicago Divinity School; Disciples Divinity House, Vanderbilt University Divinity School; and Disciples Seminary Foundation, School of Theology at Claremont and Pacific School of Religion.

[3] Tier I grants from Disciples affiliated seminaries are:

"A Study of Quality in Ministry," Lexington Theological Seminary "Update and Revision of the Theological School Inventory," Cardwell, Sue Webb, (Christian Theological Seminary)

"Improving Recruitment and Selection of Ministerial Candidates," Phillips Graduate Seminary

"Changes in Ministerial Candidates: A 25 Year Study," Stone, Howard (Brite Divinity School)

[4] The other twelve are: Board for Theological Education, The Episcopal Church; Board of Higher Education, Mennonite Church; Colgate Rochester Divinity School; Committee on Theological Education, Presbyterian Church (USA); Evangelical Lutheran Church in America; Harvard University Divinity School; Hebrew Union College and Jewish Theological Seminary; Pacific School of Religion; Southern Baptist Theological Seminary; The United Methodist Church; Vanderbilt University Divinity School; and Washington Theological Union. A year later the Interdenominational Theological Center and the National Catholic Education Association received grants.

[5] Clergy Supply Study, an unpublished report produced by the Pension Fund of the Christian Church (Disciples of Christ), 1986, pp. 1-4.

[6] *Yearbook and Directory of the Christian Church (Disciples of Christ) 1989*, p. 170.

[7] Based on fall enrollment data compiled by the Division of Higher Education from 1979-1989. Also see *Fact Book on Theological Education 1987-88*. (Vandalia, OH: Association of Theological Schools in the United States and Canada, 1988), pp. 8-12.

[8] Steering Committee Members:

Joyce B. Coalson, Executive, Department of Ministry, Division of Homeland Ministries

John R. Foulkes, Deputy General Ministry and Vice President for Inclusive Ministries

W. Clark Gilpin, immediate past Chair, Council on Theological Education, Division of Higher Education; formerly Dean Disciples Divinity House, University of Chicago Divinity School currently Dean, University of Chicago Divinity School

122   Discerning the Call

John M. Imbler, Vice President, Division of Higher Education and Lilly Grant Project Director

Lester D. Palmer, President, Pension Fund of the Christian Church and Chair, General Board Task Force on Ministry

Nathan S. Smith, Regional Minister and President, Christian Church (Disciples of Christ) in Illinois-Wisconsin and formerly Chair, Committee on Ministry, Conference of Regional Ministers and Moderators

Linda K. Plengemeier, formerly Administrative Assistant to the Vice Presidents currently Treasurer of the Division of Higher Education, serves as staff support and fiscal manager.

James I. Spainhower, President of the Division of Higher Education, serves as Project Consultant.

[9]Don S. Browning, Alexander Campbell Professor of Religion and Psychological Studies, University of Chicago Divinity School; Team Leader

Sue Webb Cardwell, Associate Professor of Psychology and Counseling, Christian Theological Seminary

William K. Fox, Sr., Assistant to the General Minister and President and Secretary to the National Convocation, Emeritus

William O. Paulsell, President, Lexington Theological Seminary

M. Jack Suggs, Emeritus Dean and Professor of New Testament, Brite Divinity School, Texas Christian University

[10]Kenneth E. Henry, Professor of Church History, Interdenominational Theological Center, Atlanta; Team Leader

A. Alton Beaver, Assistant Dean and Assistant Professor of Applied Theology, Phillips Graduate Seminary, Enid, OK

William E. Crowl, Executive Regional Minister, Christian Church (Disciples of Christ) Central Rocky Mountain Region and Christian Church of Utah

Karen Knodt, Campus Minister, Southern Illinois University-Carbondale

Kenneth L. Teegarden, General Minister and President, Emeritus, Christian Church (Disciples of Christ)

[11]Holly McKissick, Pastor-Developer, Christian Church in Greater Kansas City, Team Leader

Allen V. Harris, Associate Minister, Park Avenue Christian Church, New York, NY

Robin E. Hedgeman, Associate Regional Pastor, Christian Church in Ohio (Disciples of Christ)

Jon A. Lacey, Campus Minister, Michigan State University, East Lansing, MI

Cynthia Guthrie Ryan, Associate Minister, First United Methodist Church, Graham, TX

[12]Susanne Johnson, Associate Dean, Perkins School of Theology, Southern Methodist University; Team Leader

Terry M. Ewing, Associate Regional Minister, Christian Church (Disciples of Christ) in Kentucky

Carol Lavery, Associate Regional Minister, Christian Church (Disciples of Christ) in Georgia

Stuart D. McLean, Associate Professor of Christian Education and Theological Ethics, Phillips Graduate Seminary, Enid, OK

W. Alan Smith, Associate Professor of Religion, Florida Southern University, Lakeland, FL

[13]Daisy L. Machado, Pastor-Developer, Iglesia Cristiana El Redentor, Houston, TX, currently a PhD student at the University of Chicago; Team Leader

Edwin L. Becker, Professor of Sociology of Religion, Emeritus, Christian Theological Seminary

Diane Jackson, Lay Minister, Central Christian Church, Indianapolis, IN

David Rodriguez, Industrial Psychologist, Citibank, New York, NY

[14]M. Margaret Harrison, Regional Minister, Christian Church (Disciples of Christ) in the Southwest; Team Leader

C. William Bryan, Associate Professor of Practical Theology and Director of Field Education, Phillips Graduate Seminary, Enid, OK

Claudia Highbaugh, Associate Chaplain, Yale University, New Haven, CT

Wm. Chris Hobgood, Executive Minister, Christian Church (Disciples of Christ) in Arkansas

Janet Johnson Riley, Family Therapist, Family Services Association, Indianapolis, IN

[15]Brian W. Grant, Associate Professor of Pastoral Care and Counseling, Christian Theological Seminary; Team Leader

Richard L. Harrison, Jr., Dean, Disciples Divinity House and Associate Professor of Church History, Vanderbilt University Divinity School

Stephen V. Sprinkle, Pastor, Pleasant Union Christian Church, Newton Grove, NC

D. Newell Williams, Associate Professor of Modern and American Church History, Christian Theological Seminary

[16]Max Weber, *The Protestant Ethic and the Spirit of Capitalism* (New York: Charles Scribner's Sons, 1958).

[17]Joseph C. Hough, Jr. and John B. Cobb, Jr., *Christian Identity and Theological Education* (Atlanta: Scholars Press, 1985).

[18]Ronald E. Osborn, *The Education of Ministers for the Coming Age* (St. Louis: Christian Board of Publication, 1987), p. 182.

[19]Barbara Wheeler and Joseph, C. Hough, Jr., *Beyond Clericalism* (Atlanta: Scholars Press, 1988).

[20]Robert Schuller, et. al. (eds.), *Ministry in America* (San Francisco: Harper and Row, 1980). See especially pages 307-331 for Disciples of Christ.

[21]The following profile is that used by the Christian Church (Disciples of Christ) in Oregon:

THE UNDERCARE PROGRAM
IN OREGON

The undercare Program is a flexible plan whereby a person may explore the opportunities and responsibilities of a career in the Order of Ministry of the Christian Church (Disciples of Christ).

Q. How do I enter the Undercare Program?

A. By filling out the form on the back of this brochure and meeting with the Commission on the Ministry.

Q. What are the continuing responsibilities under the Program?

A. 1. You need to read the Policies and Criteria for the Order of Ministry in the Christian Church (Disciples of Christ), available from the Regional Office.

2. Write an annual statement of your progress toward the ministry.

3. Meet with the Commission on the Ministry once each year.
4. Let the Department know, in writing, if you decide not to enter the ministry.

Q. How old should I be to enter the Program?

A. There is no set age for entrance. A person may enter the Program when a junior or senior in high school. A person may enter the Program late in life.

Q. What are some of the main purposes of the Program?

A. It establishes an official relationship between you and the Region; it can support you; it offers encouragement; it provides a method for communicating; it begins the process of structures supervision which all clergy persons experience; it provides answers for continued personal and spiritual growth.

Q. Will I receive a lot of mail?

A. The Program depends largely on *your* initiative. When you have questions or needs, let the commission know. Commission members are here to help.

Q. If I enter the Program, must I then become a minister?

A. No. The Program is low-key. It is intended to assist you in making the proper decision for you not forcing you into a decision which will be good

for no one.

Q. What are the region's responsibilities?

A. To assign a commission member as a contact person for you.
   2. To see to it that the regional minister ia available for you.
   3. To provide factual information describing possibilities and limits.
   4. To answer qestions clearly.
   5. To be a resource for counsel, support, encouragement, and concern.

CHRISTIAN CHURCH (DISCIPLES OF CHRIST) IN OREGON

COMMISSION ON THE MINISTRY APPLICATION FOR UNDERCARE PROGRAM

Purpose of the Undercare Program: To establish and continue a relationship between the Regional Church and persons contemplating the minister as a career.

1. Name

   Phone

   Address

   Birth date/Birth place

   Marital Status (spouse's name)

2. I am a member of the Christian Church (Disciples of Christ) Yes___ No___

Local congregation

Address

Pastor

3. Schools, colleges, seminaries, graduate schools attended.

4. Work Experience:

5. My plans: ( ) I plan to explore the ministry ( ) I plan to become a minister ( ) I plan to attend seminary ( ) I have not decided to enter the ministry.

6. Three persons the Department may contact concerning me:

7. I understand that my obligation involves continuing communication with the Commission. I understand that the Undercare Program does not oblige me to enter ministry.

Signature_____ date

Pastor: Please write remarks here if you care to make any:

Pastor _____ date

Chair _____ date

Regional Minister _____ date

[22]Supported through contributions by African-American individuals, congregations, and the National Convocation of the Christian Church (Disciples of Christ), the Star Supporter Fund is a scholarship program administered by the Department of Ministry of the Division of Homeland Ministries for Black seminarians and undergraduate students preparing for Christian ministry.

[23]Lexington Theological Seminary, May 1989 in cooperation with the Christian Church in Kentucky performed this study through a Lilly Endowment, Inc. Tier I Grant.

[24]Short Term Employment Experience in Ministry, sponsored by the Division of Higher Education, is a ten week summer intern program for racial/ethnic minorities to "test" their calls to ministry through a variety of ministerial experiences with congregations, church-related institutions, general units, or regional camping programs.

[25]See *Practical Theology: The Emerging Field in Theology, Church, and the World*, edited by Don Browning, for this critique. *Ministry for the Coming Age* by Ronald Osborn, and the work of James Hopewell, Alice and Robert Evans, and others, also suggest that the church needs to rethink its assumptions that ministry is vested primarily within the ordained clergy.

[26]H. Richard Niebuhr, *Christ and Culture* (New York: Harper and Brothers, 1951).

[27]Dean Hoge, "Five Differences Between Black and White Protestant Youth," *Affirmation*, (Spring 1989), p. 75.

[28]Deborah Finn, "Is Rock Music a Poor Source of Values?" *The Disciple*, (November 1986), p. 53.

126 Discerning the Call

[29] Charlie Gillett, *The Sound of the City: The Rise of Rock and Roll* (New York: Outerbridge & Dienstrey, 1970), p. vi.

[30] Greil Marcus, *Lipstick Traces: A Secret History of the Twentieth Century* (Cambridge: Harvard University Press, 1989).

[31] Andrew Greeley, *God in Popular Culture* (Chicago: Thomas More Press, 1988), p. 9.

[32] Unexpected life events are *un*scheduled crises, such as the premature death of a loved one. Some crises are *mis*scheduled (teenage pregnancy) or *over*scheduled (a gay adult forcing himself to marry out of social pressure).

[33] cf. *Effective Christian Education: A National Study of Protestant Congregations -A Report to the Christian Church (Disciples of Christ)*, (Minneapolis, MN: 1990) [Hereafter referred to as Search Institute, *Ibid.*; and David Elkind, *All Grown Up and No Place to Go: Teenagers in Crisis*, (Reading, MA: Addison-Wesley Publishing Co., 1984).

[34] Search Institute, *Ibid.*, p. 23.

[35] Kenneth L. Woodward, "Young Beyond Their Years," *Newsweek*, Special Edition, (Winter/Spring 1990), p. 60.

[36] Hoge, *Ibid.*, p. 82.

[37] Charles R. Foster, "The High School and Youth Ministry: A Critical Perspective," *The Living Light* (January 1989), p. 141.

[38] This is the title of a nearly completed book by Stuart D. McLean.

[39] See Robin Maas, "What Language Shall We Borrow? Talking To and About God," *Affirmation*, (Spring 1989), pp. 27-36; also see Susanne Johnson, *Christian Spiritual Formation* (Nashville: Abingdon Press, 1989).

[40] H. Richard Niebuhr, Daniel Day Williams, and James M. Gustafson, *The Purpose of the Church and Its Ministry: Reflections on the Aims of Theological Education* (New York: Harper, 1956).

[41] Search Institute, *Ibid.*, p. 23.

[42] *Ibid.*, p. 41.

[43] Elkind, *Ibid.*, p. 143.

[44] Search Institute, *Ibid.*, p. 56.

[45] *Ibid.*, p. 41.

[46] *Ibid.*, p. 23.

[47] *Ibid.*, p. 42.

[48] *Ibid.*, p. 56.

[49] *Ibid.*, p. 24.

[50] *Ibid.*, pp. 2-3.

[51] Edwin Becker was assigned the responsibility of preparing drafts of our report.

[52] Activities and attempts in this direction through the general church are described in the section "The Present Situation and Future Prospects of These Groups Among Disciples" beginning on page 85.

[53] Strategy Research Corporation, *S.T.A.R. Surveys*, p. 361.

[54] Justo Gonzales. *The Theological Education of Hispanics*, a study commissioned by the Fund for Theological Education, New York, NY, 1988. p. 21.

[55] Strategy Research Corporation, *S.T.A.R. Surveys*, pages 361 and 363.

[56] Gonzales, *Ibid.*, p. 50.

[57] *The Christian Church (Disciples of Christ) Profile of the Black Ministers, the Black Church Congregations and Facilities*, by Irving H. Allen, Sr., Ph.D., sponsored by The Division of Homeland Ministries and The Division of Higher Education of the Christian Church (Disciples of Christ), 1985, p. 44.

[58] *Ibid.*, p. 45.

[59]*Ibid.*, p. 23.
[60]*Ibid.*, p. 77.
[61]*Ibid.*, p. 46.
[62]*Ibid.*, p. 73.
[63]Report of Star Supporter Grants for years 1976-1988, Department of Ministry, Division of Homeland Ministries.
[64]Report on the Hispanic Scholarship Fund, 1982-1990, Department of Ministry, Division of Homeland Ministries.
[65]See report, "Asian Ministries Consultation," October 12-14, 1989, Techny Conference Center, Chicago, Illinois. Sponsored by Division of Homeland Ministries, Christian Church (Disciples of Christ). Present were seven general church staff, three regional church staff, seven congregational clergy, two chaplains, one seminary dean, and three lay leaders.
[66]Refer to Chapter Seven for further evidence of this position.
[67]*Fact Book on Theological Education*, 1987-88, *Ibid.*, pp. 10-11.
[68]Professor of theology at Christian Theological Seminary, Clark Williamson met with the Study Team in January 1990. This comment reflects a presentation he make to the team at that time.
[69]Participants in the October 1-3 Planning Conference are listed below with vocational and regional designations. The team numbers in parentheses identify those who served on the various study teams that prepared the resource document.

William Bryan (team 7), Seminary Professor, Oklahoma
LaTaunya Bynum, General Unit Staff, Indiana
Tim Carson, Pastor, Mid-America
Janet Casey-Allen, Juvenile Chaplain, Indiana
Howard Cavner, Campus Minister, Mid-America
William Drake, Seminary Administrator, Kentucky
Terry Ewing (team 4), Associate Regional Minister, Kentucky
Sheryl Fancher, Clergy Career Consultant, Kansas
Brian Grant (team 1), Seminary Professor, Indiana
Owen Guy, Minister of Christian Education, Tennessee
Robert Harris, Pastor, Indiana
Margaret Harrison (team 7), Regional Minister, Southwest
Kenneth Henry (team 6), Seminary Professor, Georgia
Diane Jackson (team 5), Lay Minister, Indiana
Susanne Johnson (team 4), Seminary Administrator, Southwest
Karen Knodt (team 6), Campus Minister, Illinois-Wisconsin
Daisy Machado (team 5), PhD Student, Illinois-Wisconsin (Southwest)
Holly McKissick (team 3), Pastor-Developer, Greater Kansas City
Samuel Pagan, Biblical Theologian, Florida
Rod Parrott, Seminary Foundation Administrator, Pacific Southwest
Tracye Ruffin, 1990 Seminary Graduate, Pastor, Arkansas
Cynthia Guthrie Ryan (team 3), Associate Minister-UM Congregation, Southwest
Edward Saywer, Undergraduate Religion Professor, Mid-America
Landa Simmons, Naval Chaplain, Florida
Steve Sprinkle (team 1), Pastor, North Carolina
Robert Steffer, Regional Minister, Canada
Jack Suggs, (team 2), Retired Seminary Professor and Dean, Southwest
Ed Weisheimer, Associate Regional Minister, Indiana
Lois Williams, Laywoman, Indiana

Ex-Officio

Joyce Coalson, Department of Ministry, Indiana
John Foulkes, Office of General Minister and President, Indiana
Richard Harrison, Chair of the Council on Theological Education, Tennessee
John Imbler, Division of Higher Education, Mid-America
Lester Palmer, Pension Fund of the Christian Church, Indiana
Linda Plengemeier, Division of Higher Education, Mid-America
James Spainhower, Division of Higher Education, Mid-America

[70]"Policies and Criteria for the Order of Ministry" are contained in the manual **The Design for the Christian Church (Disciples of Christ) and General Rules and Policies**, produced by the Office of the General Minister and President, (Indianapolis, 1989), pp. 37f.

[71]The Missouri School of Religion offers short-term and week-end courses on-site and at off-campus locations on specific topics of interest and value to individuals and the church. Instructors are practitioners in their fields. More information on programs and schedules may be obtained from the Missouri School of Religion, P.O. Box 104685, Jefferson City, Missouri, 65110-4685.

[72]In addition to the Christian Church (Disciples of Christ), the other COCU denominations are: African Methodist Episcopal Church, African Methodist Episcopal Zion Church, Christian Methodist Episcopal Church, Episcopal Church, International Council of Community Churches, Presbyterian Church (USA), United Church of Christ, and United Methodist Church. The Lutheran Council in the USA, Reformed Church in America, and Roman Catholic Church sit on COCU's Theology Commission as Observers/Consultants.

Bibliography

Allen, Irving H. Sr. *The Christian Church (Disciples of Christ) Profile of the Black Ministers, the Black Church Congregations and Facilities*. Sponsored by The Division of Homeland Ministries and The Division of Higher Education of the Christian Church (Disciples of Christ) in cooperation with Jarvis Christian College, Hawkins, Texas. 1985.

Asian Ministers Consultation, Report of a meeting sponsored by the Division of Homeland Ministries of the Christian Church (Disciples of Christ), October 12-14, 1989.

Browning, D., Evison, I., and Polk, D. (eds.) *The Education of the Practical Theologian*. Scholars Press, 1989.

Browning, Don (ed.). *Practical Theology: The Emerging Field in Theology, Church, and World*. Harper and Row, 1983.

Browning, Don. "Spiritual and Intellectual Qualities for Ministerial Leadership of the Future" (manuscript), 1989.

Brueggeman, Walter. *The Creative Word*. Fortress Press, 1982.

CAN Church Advance Now, Evaluation Report: Board of Church Extension of the Christian Church Extension of the Christian Church (Disciples of Christ), July 28, 1989.

Cardwell, Sue. "Quality of Ministerial Leadership" (manuscript), 1989.

Directorio Ministerios Hispanos Iglesia Cristiana (Discipulos de Cristo) en los Estados Unidos Y Canada 1988-1989. La Oficina de Ministerios Hispanos, Departmento de Evangelismo, Division de Ministerios Domesticos, Indianapolis, Indiana.

Effective Christian Education: A National Study of Protestant Congregations—A Report for the Christian Church (Disciples of Christ). Search Institute, 1990.

Elkind, David. *All Grown Up and No Place to Go: Teenagers in Crisis*. Addison-Wesley Publishing Co., 1984.

Fox, William. "Some Observations from the Perspective of the Black Experience and/or Denominational Agencies" (manuscript), 1989.

Gillett, Charles. *"The Sound of the City:" The Rise of Rock and Roll*. Outerbridge & Dienstry, 1970.

Gonzales, Justo L. *The Theological Education of Hispanics*. The Fund for Theological Education, New York, 1988.

Greeley, Andrew. *God in Popular Culture*. Thomas More Press, 1988.

Greil, Marcus. *Lipstick Traces: A Secret History of the Twentieth Century*. Harvard University Press, 1989.

Hough, Joseph. and Cobb, John. *Christian Identity and Theological Education*. Scholars Press, 1985.

McLean, Stuart D. "Rites of Passage Youth Ministry: An Alternative" (manuscript to be published).

Messer, Donald. *Contemporary Images of Christian Ministry*. Abingdon, 1989.

Miller, Don and Poling, James. *Foundations for a Practical Theology of Ministry*. Abingdon, 1985.

Mudge, Lewis and Poling, James (eds.). *Formation and Reflection: The Promise of Practical Theology*. Fortress, 1987.

Niebuhr, H. Richard. *Christ and Culture*. Harper and Brothers, 1951.

Osborn, Ronald, *The Education of Ministers for the Coming Age*. Christian Board of Publication, 1987.

Paulsell, William. "Qualifications for Ministry in the Area of Spirituality" (manuscript), 1989.

Strategy Research Corporation, *U. S. Hispanic Market Study*. New York, NY. 1989.

Schuller, Robert (ed.). *Ministry in America*. Harper and Row, 1980.

Suggs, Jack. "New Testament Criteria" (manuscript), 1989.

Weber, Max. *The Protestant Ethic and the Spirit of Capitalism*. Charles Scribner's Sons, 1958.

Wheeler, Barbara and Hough, Joseph. *Beyond Clericalism*. Scholars Press, 1988.